THE ULTIMATE GUIDE
TO BECOMING A

FASHION MAKEUP ARTIST

CHRISTABEL DRAFFIN

Copyright © 2021, Christabel Draffin

christabeldraffin.com
@christabeldraffin

All rights reserved.
No part of this book may be reproduced or transmitted in any form or by any means, electronic or mechanical, including photocopying, recording or by any information storage and retrieval system without written permission of the publisher.

Cover Design: Johnny Richards   •   *johnnyrichards.com*
Cover Photograph: Kellie French   •   *kelliefrench.com*
Layout design: Lazar Kackarovski

ISBN: 979-8-500796-48-6

Imprint: Independently published

To my Dad,
who never doubted
that one day I would write.

DISCLAIMER

This book details the author's personal experiences with and opinions about becoming a fashion makeup artist. The author is not a financial advisor or a healthcare provider.

Except as specifically stated in this book, neither the author or publisher, nor any contributors, will be liable for damages arising out of or in connection with the use of this book. This is a comprehensive limitation of liability that applies to all damages of any kind, including (without limitation) compensatory; direct, indirect or consequential damages; loss of income or profit; loss of or damage to property and claims of third parties. Every person's situation is different and the advice and strategies contained herein might not be suitable for your situation. You understand that this book is not intended as a substitute for consultation with a licensed healthcare practitioner or a licensed financial advisor or tax attorney. This book provides some content related to health and/or financial issues. As such, use of this book implies your acceptance of this disclaimer.

TABLE OF CONTENTS

Introduction 11

Section 1: **Getting started**   19

  Chapter 1:   **Choosing your Makeup Direction and Being Intentional** 20

            Areas of Makeup You Can Work
            – Session Work and Non-Session Work . . . 21

            Cross-over Between Makeup Fields 23

  Chapter 2:   **How to Build Your Portfolio** 25

            Shooting Tests 26

            Getting in Touch with People. 27

            How to Decide What to Shoot 29

            Once You've Found Creatives to Shoot With . 29

            Where to Shoot – Studio or Location 30

            Getting Published 31

            Submissions 32

            Commissioned Editorial 32

            Go-Sees. 33

            Shooting for Online or Print?. 34

Chapter 3:	**Preparing to Shoot**	**35**
	Production	35
	Booking Models	35
	Choosing the Rest of the Team	36
	Other Things to Organise	36
	Shoot the Story	37
	Mood Boards	37
	Fashion References	38
	Getting the Images from the Photographer	39
	Organising and Storing Your Images	39
	Do It All Again, But Do It Better	40
	Finding Your Style	41
	Portfolio vs iPad	42
	Putting Your Portfolio in Order	43
	Basic Portfolio Rules	44
Chapter 4:	**How to Build Your Website**	**46**
	Getting Started	46
	Video and Moving Image	48
	Do I Need a Website If I Have Instagram?	48
Chapter 5:	**Social Media**	**49**
	Instagram	49
	Instagram Tips	50
	Building Community	52
	Using Instagram Stories/Reels	54
	A Final Note on Instagram	55
	Other Social Media Platforms	56

Section 2:	*Getting out there*	59
Chapter 6:	**Assisting**	61
	What Skills You Need for Assisting	62
	How to be a Great Assistant	63
	Benefits of Assisting	65
	How Do I Get Assisting Work?	66
	Getting Assisting Work Through an Agency	66
	Getting Assisting Work Directly through an Artist	68
	How to Send the Right Email to an Agency	69
	What to Have in an Assisting Makeup Kit	70
	High Level Assisting	71
	Do I Need to Assist?	72
	Know Your History	72
Chapter 7:	**Relationships and Networking**	73
	How to Build Your Network	74
	Keeping in Touch with your Network	74
	Recommending Other Creatives	75
	Building Relationships with Photographers	75
	Building Relationships with Makeup Brands and How Beauty PR Works	76
	Makeup Artist Credit Programmes	77
Chapter 8:	**Working for Free**	79
	How to Decide When It's Worth Working for Free	81
	How Long Do I Need to Work for Free?	82
	Non-Makeup Jobs You Can Do Whilst You Build Your Makeup Career	82

Section 3: Money — 84

Chapter 9: Making Money 85
- Makeup Artist Day Rates 86
- Paid Work 86
- Commercial Rates 86
- Editorial Rates. 87
- Negotiate Your Rate on a Commercial Job . . 89
- How to Get Your First Client 90
- Working for the Music Industry 91
- Invoicing 91
- Chasing Late Invoices 92
- The Types of Makeup Work You Can Do to Earn Money as a Makeup Artist . . . 93

Chapter 10: Managing Your Expenses 110
- Controlling Your Expenses 110
- Budgeting — Your Basic Budget 111
- Budgeting Software 111
- Having an Emergency Fund 112
- Creating a Kit Budget 114
- Buying Foundations 115
- Cheaper Makeup Ranges 116
- A Final Recommendation 116

Chapter 11: Taxes and Insurance 118
- Paying Taxes 118
- Putting Money Aside to Pay Tax 118
- Track Your Expenses for Your Taxes 119
- Insurance for Makeup Artists 119

Section 4: Looking Ahead — **121**

Chapter 12: Time Management and Organisation . . . **122**
- *Analysing What's Working* 125
- *Always Say Yes* 126
- *Being Organised* 126
- *Managing Your Kit* 127
- *Preparation for Work* 128
- *Fitting It All In* 129

Chapter 13: Managing your Health **131**
- *Looking After Your Health at Work* 132
- *Decant your Kit* 134
- *Managing Burnout* 135

Chapter 14: Getting an Agent **137**
- *Benefits of Having an Agent* 138
- *Negatives of Having an Agent* 138
- *Tips for Getting an Agent* 139
- *How Do I Know I'm Ready for an Agent?* . . . 141
- *Is It Possible to Be Successful Without an Agent?* 143

Section 5: Dealing with different life circumstances — **145**

- *I Already Have a Full-Time Job – Can I Transition to Becoming a Makeup Artist?* 146
- *What if I Have Already Left My Job to Become a Makeup Artist?* 148
- *How Do I Bring in Work When the Industry is Quiet?* 149
- *I Can't Pay My Bills This Month, What Should I Do?* 151

I've Had a Career Setback –
  What Do I do to Snap Out of It?. 153

How Do I Come Back to Makeup Work
  After a Break? 154

How Do I Manage Makeup Work
  if I Have Kids? 155

Makeup Is a Second Career for me –
  Am I Too Old? 157

I Don't Live in a Capital City
  – Can I Still Be a Makeup Artist? 158

Section 6: The road ahead   160

Keeping Up Your Confidence
  – the Mental Game. 161

You're On Your Way 164

Acknowledgements 165

INTRODUCTION

Over the last couple of years I have received so many messages every week from aspiring makeup artists who are trying to figure out how to get the ball rolling on their dreamed of career, and I realised it's just as hard now to start as an editorial fashion makeup artist as it was when I began, two decades ago.

I want to share the hidden tricks of what I've learnt about becoming a makeup artist, so you don't have to go through the painful process of working it all out on your own. The aim of this book is to help fill in all the gaps and missing pieces about HOW to build that much-dreamed of career that only a successful, working makeup artist can tell you – about what works, and what doesn't, so you can learn from my mistakes.

In early 2020, the COVID-19 coronavirus hit the world. No country will come out of this unscathed, and likewise the world's citizens. I can't see into the future, but I do know that fashion, like every industry, will be radically affected. This made me wonder whether the world needed this book about becoming a makeup artist, if we're going into such a difficult and radically shifting time. After considerable thought, I decided this information would be more useful than ever as everything in life has just got that much harder and you will need as much knowledge as possible to carve out your path as a makeup artist moving forward.

I'm a huge believer in not having regrets in life – if you don't try being a makeup artist, you will never know if it's for you or not. However good planning and a thorough understanding of what is involved with becoming a working makeup artist BEFORE making the leap is very important. And if I can explain to you the basic process of building a fashion makeup career, you can decide if this sounds like it's for you.

Why this book?

It's designed for those of you who are in the process of either becoming a makeup artist or wanting to become a makeup artist. This I totally understand as it's a desire I had for much of my life (makeup was a second career for me.)

Prior to getting an agent, I had to teach myself sales, promotion and social media marketing in order to get makeup work that pays. Eventually I built a satisfying creative career that allows me now to work in London on advertising, with celebrities and do regular editorials for magazines like Vogue, Harper's Bazaar, W, Vanity Fair, L'Uomo Vogue, ELLE and L'Officiel.

Even though now there are so many more resources for learning about becoming a fashion makeup artist, from YouTube, to podcasts and interviews with those artists who have 'made it', I still found most of the information didn't break down the actual steps to building the career that you want – to earning money as a makeup artist and the tangible process required to get there. Too many interviews with successful makeup artists in the business glossed over HOW they actually did it. And thus, this book was born to address this issue.

What this Book ISN'T

This book is NOT about how to apply makeup – there are many great courses and makeup schools available all over the world, as well as websites, books and YouTube videos from working makeup artists (such as Lisa Eldridge) that can help you with that.

This book also doesn't cover becoming a makeup artist for film, television or theatre, as these are all quite separate industries. However, most of the principles that I discuss with regards to marketing and building a solid financial foundation for yourself would definitely help with building a career in those areas too.

It's a guide to the process of becoming a fashion makeup artist, how to build a business that can sustain and support you and allow you to do the type of makeup that you want. Fashion makeup is quite a specialised field and is highly, highly competitive. It can be very difficult to break into without contacts and/or knowledge about how to do it. You'll be pleased to know that I didn't have any special contacts in the industry when I started, no fashion fairy godmother to help me out!

A Secretive and Competitive Industry

Like any business, makeup IS competitive – it's naïve to think that it isn't. Fashion makeup is even more so.

Even if you've studied at a makeup school, many of them don't really cover what comes next after your course finishes. You have the necessary makeup skills, a newly purchased (and expensive!) kit and often very little idea about business-wise what to do next.

It's very hard to find out about salaries in fashion and because it's a competitive and ever-changing industry, the people already working in it are less likely to share fee information about what they get paid for different jobs. It's such a difficult industry to break into that not everyone is open to sharing secrets.

But then as no-one talks about it, how do you find out about the practicalities of it and not just what to do, but whether you think it's really a long-term career plan for you? Answers to questions like:

- How do I build a portfolio?
- Do I still need a website?
- Do I need Instagram?
- How do I support myself whilst I build my portfolio and network?
- Should I assist other makeup artists?
- How do I get assisting work?
- How do I get my first client?
- How do I get more work?
- How do I get an agent?

These are all the questions (and more) I want to answer for you in this guide.

My belief is that a rising tide raises all boats. Without getting all *'The Secret'* on you, the more we help each other and give from an abundant place the greater that I believe we all benefit. I also think not knowing how the process of building a makeup career works could potentially stop people from pursuing it at all which I think is a shocking waste.

The global fashion industry has been shifting a lot in the last few years. Everything has been changing so rapidly that just keeping up with all the developments is difficult, let alone increasing your income and keeping the level at which you are working improving. There are more and more people starting out in the creative industries all the time, thus competition is rapidly growing, making it harder to stand out from other artists. Also the nature of the work in fashion has changed with many more shoots for online publications and brands which has tended to reduce what the creative people who work on those shoots are getting paid overall.

However, having said that there has never been a better time in history to show your work or utilise the opportunity that we've been afforded by the internet. There have never been as many work possibilities available, you can now control all your own marketing and sales process and it's never been easier to connect with other people in the industry and get the ball rolling on your career. Being able to navigate the current landscape both as a new makeup artist and as an established artist is more important than ever, and the ability to effectively promote yourself online is a really key differentiator between success and failure.

There are also other things that have made it easier to be a makeup artist, in that as traditional print magazine titles keep closing, there has been a huge surge in independent online publishing and there are many more platforms from all over the world (both print and online) to showcase your work. It's also never been cheaper to build a kit with dozens of great brands out there at a much more affordable price point than in the past, and the quality of makeup products now has also vastly improved with better formulations.

My argument is that as long as people are wearing and buying clothes, which unless total nudity becomes popular (something I don't see happening anytime soon), there will always be work for good fashion makeup artists. Fashion globally was worth $1.34 trillion a year as of 2019, so there is still money in this business, and your job is to go get it, and get paid for doing makeup.

There is an economic barometer of consumer confidence called 'the Lipstick Index', and even in times of economic uncertainty and recession, sales of lipstick and beauty products go up as they are small purchases that are a little bit of luxury and they are relatively inexpensive. No matter what is happening with the economy, there will always be room for feeling good with makeup.

The other reason I wrote this book is because I hate the exploitation side of fashion – being a fashion creative is spectacularly unregulated and unfortunately there are a lot of people wanting free or cheap labour from creatives (makeup artists/stylists/hairdressers/photographers) in exchange for giving them 'exposure'. Whilst I understand that there will always be an element of working for free inherent in being a makeup artist (since we do have to shoot regular editorial for free to showcase our work – more on this later), there are definitely unscrupulous people and companies who are happy to get makeup artists' hard work without paying for it.

This doesn't mean that I think you can charge for every job that you do right from the word go either – makeup is a trade or craft, and like every trade or craft you DO need to build a solid foundation of hours on-set, much of which will be unpaid at the beginning. But there is a line between work that is beneficial to you and work that is exploiting you, and I'd like you to know the difference. Knowledge is power!

ABOUT ME

I grew up in Sydney, Australia and when I was a teenager I fell in love with fashion from the minute I found a copy of American ELLE. I loved everything about the glamorous world of Vogue and Harper's Bazaar and dreamed that I would one day be part of that sphere.

Whilst I was at Sydney University studying English literature, I did a weekend course in makeup, but it was makeup for films (like most of the makeup courses at the time.) I decided that special effects and wig creation was not for me and went to London where I worked in PR and then communications marketing for a few years.

I met my French husband in London and getting sick of the cold, we decided it was time to move back to Sydney. Along with the move I realised I wanted a career change as well, and having discovered that you could do makeup for fashion and just make people look beautiful, I thought I'd give makeup another try. I did a short refresher course in fashion makeup and started assisting pretty much straight away after calling the local Sydney agencies to say I was available.

I also began building my makeup portfolio by testing with any photographer I could find. Very soon after I started assisting, I found out I was pregnant. I had terrible morning sickness in my pregnancy so I couldn't work much and then spent the first couple of years at home with my son which was great, just doing shoots when I could sort out childcare.

On holiday in Europe when my son was eighteen months old, I figured I had nothing to lose so I took my new leather portfolio (we had massive leather bound portfolios to show our work in those days) and literally knocked on the door of Streeters Agency in London who represented Pat McGrath, who was my favourite makeup artist in the world at the time. I wouldn't dream of that now, but at the time I had no idea this wasn't the done thing, and in a very Australian manner I just thought "I'll give it a go".

It worked, and I was lucky enough to be asked to assist on Pat's shows the next season. Unfortunately, due to my husband's new job I couldn't go to Europe at that time, but it made me realise what was possible.

We moved to Paris soon after. When we were settled, I literally went agency door knocking again, this time arriving on the doorstep of Jed Root which was in those days one of the world's best creative fashion agencies. I met an amazing agent there who called me back that afternoon to ask if I could go to iconic photographer Paolo

Roversi's studio to assist English makeup artist Alex Box for two days as she needed a bi-lingual assistant to translate for her.

That was the beginning of everything for me as it opened my eyes to high-fashion makeup – I learnt more from Alex in Paris in two days than in all my years of doing makeup in Australia. It also told me that the best things happen when you least expect it, always be ready, and always say yes to anything and everything when you're starting out. You never know where a job might lead!

There were plenty of rejections as well along the way, so it wasn't all smooth sailing. I vividly remember a humiliating conversation with one of the agents at another Paris agency who literally laughed in my face that I wanted to assist one of their makeup artists. For every positive response there are always a lot of knockbacks and it's something you need to get used to - which happens by constantly contacting people and not getting disheartened. It's all part of the process.

A quick note – I really wouldn't recommend literally knocking on agencies' doors like I did. When I think back on it now, I totally cringe. Especially as there are so many ways to contact agencies with emails and social media, I think it would do you more harm than good to actually turn up on the agency doorstep. Don't forget it was many years ago when I did this, and times have moved on.

We ended up settling in London a couple of years later. Because of the job I did in Paris with Alex Box, when I arrived in London I contacted her agency at the time (called D&V Management) which had a really cool roster of top artists.

D&V then put me on Alex's fashion show team, and on the show teams for some of their other makeup artists. Then after fashion week that season, I started assisting on shoots with their other artists: Advertising, editorial (most of it unpaid, at least to start with), music videos, shows and celebrity jobs - for a number of years I worked with their roster of makeup artists, including Alex, Sam Bryant, Florrie White and Lisa Butler, and was eventually taken on as Kay Montano's 'First Assistant'.

Kay is the most amazing makeup artist with a career that spans over thirty years. She has worked with the complete who's who of fashion photographers including Steven Meisel, Helmut Newton, Patrick Demarchelier, Ellen von Unwerth, Steven Klein, Annie Leibovitz, David Bailey, Ryan McGinley, Mario Sorrenti, Bruce Weber and Corinne Day to name a few, as well as practically any celebrity you can think of. She was a makeup artist whose work had totally inspired me for years, so I was beyond thrilled when she asked me after a show to be her first ever First Assistant.

D&V also started giving me overflow work when they had small jobs that one of their makeup artists couldn't do. This overflow work usually paid an assisting fee which was less than one of their regular makeup artists would charge, but great to be getting paid something whilst building my own portfolio and client list. Sort of makeup training wheels if you like! It gave me experience of bigger jobs and clients but without the pressure of handling on my own the type of big budget jobs that artists like Kay and Sam Bryant were doing.

For a few years I assisted as much as I could on shoots and shows – still really having zero idea about the business side of things but learning so much about the dynamics of shoots. Then one year I had a major muscle injury at London Fashion Week from carrying too much kit and standing up too much. One operation in London later and I still wasn't better, so my husband and I decided to go back to Sydney where I had yet another operation. This one worked, and we stayed in Australia for about five years until my husband got transferred with work back to London.

About a year after arriving back in London I got my London agent, and since then I have been working as a fashion makeup artist on magazine editorial, advertising, celebrity, and red carpet work. You can see my path to becoming a makeup artist wasn't straightforward at all, no overnight success or special family fashion connections. If I had one secret to becoming a makeup artist it's really just perseverance - keeping on going, even when things are hard, as they are from time to time. If you can get up and keep going after a setback, eventually you will get to where you want to go.

SECTION ONE
Getting started

CHAPTER 1

Choosing your Makeup Direction and Being Intentional

When you are first starting out as a freelance fashion makeup artist, it can be a bit overwhelming if you aren't sure what direction you want to go in with your makeup work. Fashion makeup can range from super-natural to the wildest avant-garde looks, from simple beauty makeup making people look gorgeous to conceptual, character-based makeup – it can be hard to focus on where you might want your career to go, especially if you haven't found your style yet (which is normal, to start with).

There are so many different areas of fashion and they can be quite varied in terms of the type of makeup that are involved and also the working hours and conditions. Each area of makeup can have a different network of people working in it and different ways to market yourself. In Chapter 9 I go into more detail about the various types of makeup work you can do to earn money, and how to go about getting that particular kind of work.

Please note that whilst going to a makeup school is not a necessity in most parts of the world, depending where you live you might need professional accreditation/licensing to work as a makeup artist. It's definitely worth checking this online for your area before you dive into the world of freelance makeup.

Areas of Makeup You Can Work

Session Work

Editorial and Advertising - Fashion

This is makeup for the fashion/clothing industry, so it could include makeup for shoots for print or online advertising, editorial for magazines, social media for brands, fashion films and TV advertising. It can include women's and menswear as well as kids' wear though some makeup artists specialise in one of these areas. (Note - editorials are full-page images in a series that tell a story on a particular theme or concept, published in print magazines or online. They can also be called a 'story' and showcase fashion, beauty or a celebrity or other person of interest.)

Editorial and Advertising - Beauty

This is makeup for the beauty industry – images of makeup, nails, wellness and hair for print and online advertising, television advertising, social media, and magazine editorial and advertorial/collaboration features. The makeup is usually photographed more close-up than when shooting fashion so thus must be completely perfect.

Runway/Fashion Shows

This is makeup for runway shows, to most effectively display a designer or brands' new clothing collection to buyers and the media.

Traditionally and prior to COVID-19, every year around the world there are two main seasons of shows for Ready to Wear for Spring/Summer and Autumn/Winter. There are also Cruise, Haute Couture and Menswear show calendars in Paris, London, New York and Milan as well as local fashion weeks such as India Fashion Week and Sydney Fashion Week. This may all change though moving forward—as of May 2020, Gucci announced that they will now only be showing twice a year and that their collections will be 'seasonless'. The pandemic looks to precipitate considerable change in this part of the industry.

Celebrity

This is makeup for celebrities for promotional public events such as a film, TV show or album premieres (often known as 'red carpet') or it could be for press events or interviews for when they release new material. It can also cover awards ceremonies like the BAFTAS, Oscars, Grammys, or promotional collaborations with brands and other celebrities or influencers.

Music Videos

Makeup for videos for artists in the music industry. There can be a lot of work available on music videos as they can involve makeup on many extras, dancers, backup singers and often involve long shoots.

Non-Session Work

Private Clients

People who want to have their makeup professionally done for events – such as parties, dinners, galas, awards ceremonies, bar and bat mitzvahs or christenings.

Bridal

Makeup for weddings - for the bride, but it can also include other members of the bridal party like the bridesmaids and mother of the bride.

Makeup Counter Work

Working for a makeup brand either on one of their counters in a department store, or their standalone makeup stores. It involves applying makeup to customers and having good product knowledge of the brand and strong sales skills. There can also be the chance to move up within the company to do makeup on shows and shoots for the brand, depending on whether that is part of their marketing strategy (MAC, NARS and Charlotte Tilbury are examples of brands that have these opportunities.)

Cross-over Between Makeup Fields

There can be some cross-over with the different areas of makeup like fashion and music videos, or fashion and celebrity covered under the umbrella of session work. Most working makeup artists do a mixture of different types of makeup work, and at some points in your career you might be more heavily involved in one area than another.

But no matter which area(s) you choose, life will be easiest for you if you focus on a couple of areas to market yourself in, even if you are working in more than two different areas. I say this because every type of makeup is generally a different market, so it can be confusing to potential clients and your followers on Instagram if you promote yourself doing runway shows one minute and then bridal the next. It's not that you can't do a mix of makeup work, but just keep them separate.

If you do makeup for fashion – such as runway, editorial, celebrity AND either a bridal or private client business, I recommend that you keep your social media accounts for both separate. Although you can always cross-promote your fashion work to your bridal or private client page, I wouldn't recommend doing it the other way around and putting brides and non-famous clients on your fashion social media accounts.

Depending on your life, circumstances, where you live, and your makeup interests you can mix the different areas of makeup to create the right career for you. Later in the book I will discuss the pros and cons of each area of makeup you can earn money in so you can start thinking about how the best combination would work for you. Of course, when you are starting out you need to try a bit of everything and it's completely alright to not know what area you want to gravitate towards. However the sooner you focus on one area, the quicker you can start getting results in it. The lovely thing about being a freelance fashion makeup artist is it's all about transferable skills.

Every makeup job you do helps you build your experience and your skills, plus giving you that super valuable on-set experience that is critical to being a successful makeup artist. By trying all different types of makeup work, you'll get a feel for whether you like it or not and whether you want more of it in future.

CHAPTER 2

How to Build Your Portfolio

n order to show your work, and showcase your abilities as a makeup artist, you need to build a portfolio. This will be your most important marketing tool.

A portfolio is a series of photographs of your work that show the type of makeup that you do, the range of your makeup skills and your general aesthetic. It used to be a physical book, and though these do still exist they can now also be an album on your phone or iPad, a website or on an Instagram page. It is what prospective clients and other creatives, such as photographers and stylists, will look at to assess your work and decide whether they think you are the right person for a particular job, or if they might like to work with you in future.

As a new makeup artist, building this is your first and most crucial task, and be warned even to get a basic portfolio together can take a reasonable amount of time. Without a portfolio you won't be taken seriously, and that's as true in Cape Town or Mumbai as in Paris or New York.

You can't build your portfolio on your own. For that, you need to build it with the help of other creatives in the fashion industry, such as photographers, stylists, models, hairdressers and set designers. There is a process for how to build your portfolio as well, and it all starts with shooting tests.

SHOOTING TESTS

The starting point to building your portfolio is to contact photographers and shoot what are called 'tests' with them. A test is a series of photographs that a creative team produce together to have images for their portfolios. In time, as your work continues to improve, these images that you shoot will start to be published in magazines (more on this later.) Everyone on the creative team is working for free in order to have those images to market their work.

Testing is a vital part of learning your craft, the dynamics of a shoot and testing yourself professionally and artistically. It allows you to check your skill level and attempt new things that you haven't tried before – different skin tones, multiple models, complex or technical makeup that might be a stretch for you, for instance. Any type of makeup that you can see by looking at magazines that you might need/want to do, can be tried out on a test before you get booked in a more pressurised environment (like a paid job) to be sure you can do it.

On a test, the photographer might be testing out a lighting setup they haven't tried before, or a new lens or type of camera, the stylist might be experimenting with a new type of clothing or brand, and the hair and makeup team might be testing out new products or a style of hair and makeup they haven't done before. Tests also tend to use newer, less experienced models who need to learn more about posing and also to get pictures for their portfolio. And in addition, the whole team are finding out what it's like to work together. You can see how vital the testing process is to build your career.

To shoot a test, you will need to arrange, at the minimum, a model and a photographer as well as yourself. In addition, if you wish to shoot fashion it's a good idea to have a stylist, who organises clothing to be there to shoot on the model on the day. As well as you doing makeup, you might also wish to have a separate hairdresser rather than doing both hair and makeup yourself. But don't think you need a huge crew or to spend a lot of money to make great pictures for your portfolio. Now with the quality of iPhones for photography and the success of shoots that people have been doing during the global coronavirus lockdown, it's amazing what can be achieved with a minimal crew and some creativity.

GETTING IN TOUCH WITH PEOPLE

In order to get those initial tests in, you need to start contacting photographers you would like to shoot with. It's a good idea to aim for photographers and stylists who do work that you like, but especially at the beginning work with as many people as you can. I always say you have to kiss a lot of frogs to get a prince, and you will need to try working with a lot of different people to discover your teams you like to consistently work with.

I find Instagram is a super useful tool for this as you can easily look at other creatives' work. When you're starting out, Instagram seems like a huge, unknowable sea of people and it's difficult to know where to begin. A good option is to visit the websites for the creative agencies in your city, and they will have a collection of artists that they represent that you can use as a starting point.

Use Google to find these agencies online. It can be a bit confusing as a Google search on 'creative agency' will bring back all kinds of advertising and PR agencies, which is not what you want, so instead put in 'Talent management + your city + makeup artist' and you should have a reasonable list to get you started. Also don't forget that you just need a single starting point for your local area – most people working in the fashion industry tag the other team members on Instagram on the shoots that they work together on, so you can quickly start to get a feel for who is working in that city, and build out a potential contact list from there.

When you are starting out, another way to find people like you who are also at the beginning of their careers is by seeking out the assistants on the bigger jobs – by doing this, you can find the assistant photographers and stylists that you will end up growing together with. They will often be tagged on Instagram on shoots that they have assisted on, so it's about doing good research.

Emailing or direct messaging photographers and stylists is usually the best place to start. Don't forget that other creatives are always looking for new people to work with and need backup hairdressers and makeup artists for when their favourite people are either away or not available. Also, other creatives, like hairdressers, are also looking for new teams to shoot with, so they can be an option to contact too.

A lot of people won't email you back, and that's OK and to be expected. Just keep track of who you have emailed so you don't accidentally contact them again later on. Eventually you will hear back from some people, and by responding to your email it opens a dialogue to hopefully working together – the starting steps to a working relationship. People might take a bit of time to get back to you and might not at all. Try not to get disheartened as it's a bit like dating, which is sometimes an easy process, and sometimes it's not. There are rejections of all types that will happen during your career, and you must remember not to take it personally. It usually has more to do with what's happening in the life of the person you're contacting than it is a reflection of your work.

It's a good idea to have some ideas of what you could shoot together, and approach photographers whose work you like. But also, be open to perhaps working with a photographer who might have a slightly different aesthetic to you, as you might find some middle ground in shooting together.

My best advice when shooting for your portfolio is to keep it simple. Whilst it is tempting to think you can copy that new Tom Ford campaign that involves a location house and hundreds of extras, if that's out of the range of the shoot budget (which is generally close to zero when you're starting out), then scale back the plans. Make it something minimal to start with and then if all goes well you can try something more elaborate in time. In my experience, the more complicated the shoot is, the less likely it is to happen.

Do research the people you are contacting properly as you would any job you were applying for. Also ensure you include working links to your Instagram and website when you message people so they can see what type of work that you do. You also need to be realistic about who you are contacting to shoot with you and try and work with creatives at your current level. There is zero point emailing top photographers like Harley Weir or Alasdair McLellan if you are just starting out as you are only wasting your time and theirs. Again it's about doing good fact-finding to figure out who is at your level to arrange who to shoot with.

HOW TO DECIDE WHAT TO SHOOT

The very first thing you need to do is decide on is what type of work/part of the market you are aiming for, so you can plan what your first couple of shoots are going to be. As you can see there are many types of shoots you could do, and especially when you're starting out you don't want to get overwhelmed. Over time, you will probably end up doing all of those types of work in one way or another, but your first job is to narrow down the options and get started.

For instance, would you love to show your close-cropped beauty work? Then focus on finding photographers on Instagram who shoot lovely beauty images. If it's fashion where your interests mainly lie, look for stylists whose work you like, and find photographers who shoot great fashion editorial.

ONCE YOU'VE FOUND CREATIVES TO SHOOT WITH

Once you've agreed to shoot with someone, there are also some things you'll want to discuss. What would you like to shoot together? Sometimes the photographer might come up with an idea, and sometimes you might have a concept you'd like to do.

Questions you might want to consider are:

- Is it fashion? (What type of fashion? Women's? Men's? Kids?)
- Is it beauty?
- Is it a test? Or is it a submission, or a commission? (More on this in a moment.)
- Where will you shoot it? Location or studio?
- Who will the stylist be?
- Are you going to do the hair, or will you get a hairdresser?
- What type of model would you like?
- What model agencies will you approach?

Obviously, the more people involved the more complex and time consuming it is to organise, but it depends on what you are planning to shoot and how much control of the shoot you want to have. If it's your idea, then you can offer more input but if it's someone else's concept it's best not to wade in too much with your opinion. The whole idea of testing is to find people you work well with and connect with, which also includes organising it as well as shooting together on the day.

Where to Shoot

Studio Shoots

This is a shoot indoors in a designated space to shoot photographs. Studios can be of all different sizes (the biggest one in London can fit multiple double decker buses!) or very small, which is fine if you are shooting beauty or portrait pictures and don't need lots of space to pull out and show the fashion.

The cost of the studio depends on the space and how nice it is – believe me, there is a big difference in the quality of studios. Some are beautiful and very well appointed, with catering on-site and multiple studio assistants to attend to every whim and need, and some are very basic in far-flung, sketchy neighbourhoods and you'll be lucky to get a working kettle to make tea. But you pay accordingly. Generally, the client or magazine you are shooting for, or whoever has the idea for the shoot, bears the studio cost. When starting out you might share the cost with the rest of the team or have a make-shift studio at home.

Location Shoots

This is when you shoot either outdoors or can mean going to a space that is not a studio to shoot 'on location'. It could be any space, indoors or outdoors, that isn't a studio.

Shoot permits from councils are needed in many outdoors locations around the world and can be very expensive. If you don't have a permit for where you are shooting, the local authorities can make you leave the area and that's the end of your shoot so it's always worth checking. However, many outdoor spaces are also free, which is obviously great if you have a super low budget.

You can also shoot on location indoors and hire or find an indoor location which could be anything from a shop, a junkyard, a gallery, to a beautiful apartment or a house. Location houses and spaces can be expensive to hire and most areas like a café/bar/restaurant will want you to pay something if you are planning to shoot there all day.

GETTING PUBLISHED

Testing is the bedrock of building your portfolio, and a great way to meet and work with other people in your local industry. However over a period of time and as your makeup skills improve, you will begin to want to see the makeup work that you are doing get published in magazines, both online and in print (paper-based) magazines. There is a process for this as well, which is detailed in this section.

SUBMISSIONS

Sometimes a test will go very well and it will be accepted by a magazine for publication in an upcoming issue. This is called shooting a submission. In order to get the story considered for publication, after the story has been shot someone from the team (usually the photographer or stylist, or it could be you) emails the final images to a list of the magazines they think might be interested in including it. If the magazine likes the story and thinks it sits well with their publication, it can be added to an upcoming issue.

COMMISSIONED EDITORIAL

Over time as you work with more experienced photographers and stylists, they will be asked to shoot what is called 'commissioned editorial'. This means a magazine has asked a photographer and/or a particular stylist to do a fashion shoot for their publication. These are almost always very low-pay, or often free shoots done by the team, for the magazine in exchange for a credit. A credit is your name being published on that shoot, in that title. You can then use this magazine title on the list of magazines you have worked on for your website and also tag the magazine on your Instagram when you use the pictures. In addition you have the option to say you used one of your favourite makeup brands, who you can then contact to get free product which I explain in depth in Chapter 7. Getting free products from brands is not guaranteed as it depends on the magazine title, but it can be a nice way to build or update your kit when it happens.

The shoot brief may come from the magazine or the photographer may be given creative license, but it means that the story will be published in that magazine title so the stylist can easily get clothes from the PR offices who lend clothing for fashion shoots. In order to do this the stylist will need what is called a Commission Letter.

Commission Letter

After the commission has been agreed, the magazine you are shooting for will give the stylist what is called a Pull letter or Commission letter so that they can borrow clothes for the shoot.

GO-SEES

As you can see, organising shoots for your portfolio can be a time consuming and laborious process. It requires a number of different contacts and elements to fall into place for it to happen, which is definitely daunting when you start out and you might well have zero contacts (that's alright! You will develop a network over time.) But good news, there is another, slightly easier way you can start shooting in the meantime.

This is to shoot 'go-sees'. A 'go-see' is when a model is sent by her agency for a meeting with a client or a photographer who wants to see what she or he looks like in person and how she/he is on camera before potentially booking them on a job. Models might have these appointments a few times a day when they aren't shooting for a full day, and at this appointment it's possible in the same way to shoot a test for you, the photographer and the model which can be great for all your portfolios.

So, it's an option as a makeup artist to arrange to do these with a photographer.

Models are usually given a 1-2-hour slot with a particular photographer, although it might be less as models are often running between castings as well. It can also be longer, but it really depends.

You will often be asked to do both hair and makeup for these, but it will generally be quick and uncomplicated. Depending on time, you might have an opportunity to do something more complex with makeup and hair. It's a good way to work with new creatives and is a lot quicker and easier to organise than a full fashion or beauty shoot.

Also, it's possible to shoot a number of models in a day which will give you variety for your portfolio.

The beauty of building a nice set of images in your portfolio means that when you start contacting companies and other photographers to offer your services, prospective clients can see exactly the type of makeup work that you do and why they should book you on an upcoming job.

SHOOTING FOR ONLINE OR PRINT?

In the past there were only print magazines, but gradually with the continual rise of internet media, many magazine titles have now moved online. They can be on a website only, or available both in print and online. Thus an 'online' or 'digital' fashion or beauty story is one that is just published on a website, as opposed to being published in a paper, print magazine.

Print magazines are still considered to be preferable to shooting exclusively for online but this is gradually changing, and shooting for online stories is becoming more and more accepted. However, print magazines still have greater kudos and are more likely to have an editorial fee that you might be paid.

The benefit of shooting for online publications is they need constant content, so it can be much easier to get an online story organised and published than one for print.

Magazine commissions for either print or online can be difficult to get, and it's very dependent on the contacts that the stylist and photographer have at different magazines. Because it's difficult, it can be tempting to just shoot tests and putting them in your portfolio and on your Instagram. There is nothing wrong with shooting those, but in time it's important to be shooting for magazines as well, as without having good magazine titles publishing your work you won't be taken seriously as you move up the industry.

CHAPTER 3

Preparing to Shoot

PRODUCTION

If you are testing or it's your concept, then you will be very much involved with organising the shoot – this is called 'producing the shoot'.

When you are more established and getting approached for work, or if it's for commercial, paid jobs, either the photographer or a producer or team of producers (depending on the size and complexity of the job) will organise the logistics of the shoot. This can involve casting the model(s), location scouting, booking the team and studio, arranging to have food for the crew to eat – there's a lot to organise when producing a shoot. Here are some of the elements you will need to consider.

BOOKING MODELS

The photographer is generally the one with the contacts at different model agencies, so they will usually arrange the model, although sometimes they will want your input on the model selection. To do this, the producer will email a number of model agencies in the city you are shooting, either requesting a specific model you have in mind or asking for suggestions of models that are available. In response the model agencies will send back emails with the available girls listed, complete with links to their portfolios and their measurements.

In the email to the model agencies, it's important to specify what it's for (test, submission, commission) and whether you have a specific type of model that you would like, if you have a preference.

CHOOSING THE REST OF THE TEAM

The photographer may already have hairdressers or stylists who they regularly work with or may want you to recommend somebody. Organising a shoot can take a couple of days or weeks depending on the complexity of what you are shooting and the team's schedules.

OTHER THINGS TO ORGANISE

The other details that will need to be organised (and will usually be done by the producer or the photographer) include:

- Finalising the date of the shoot
- Booking the location or studio
- Confirming the model that you will be shooting with
- Confirming all members of the creative team
- Organising food for the team (breakfast, lunch, coffee, tea and water – depending on the shoot time/location)
- Producing a call sheet. (The call sheet is a document stating the planned shoot location and time for the job in question and the details of all the crew with their relevant phone numbers. It can also include any other transport details or health and safety information required for the shoot day. It ensures that everyone on the team knows the logistical details for the shoot.)

SHOOT THE STORY

Once everything is in place and you have the team and model(s) booked, you can shoot the story.

MOOD BOARDS

A mood board is a number of images that have been put together into what is known as a 'board' that indicates in pictures the look and feel of the suggested story. The images can come from the magazine or client, the photographer and/or stylist or with contributions from the whole team. Sometimes these suggested images are called 'references'. If it's a commercial it will be the client's idea translated by an art director.

A mood board can range from a single page of images for everything, or more detailed information over a number of pages, showing pictorial examples of the lighting, model poses, props and hair/makeup/nail references over a multi-page emailable document. Obviously, fashion photography is a visual field and it's much easier to have pictures of the idea that you have rather than describing it or thinking the rest of the team understand what's in your head.

A mood board also gets sent as a pitch document to a potential magazine so they can approve it before the fashion shoot can take place.

How to Create a Mood Board

Creating a mood board involves selecting pictures and putting them together into an emailable document. If you want to lay them out using software, *Canva.com* is a good option.

For makeup ideas it could be looking at shoots from different magazines that are similar to what you want to do, or historical pictures, film stills or colour swatches. Mood boards can be enjoyable, but they can be very time consuming to do well. They are usually at least a couple of hours work but it does help refine ideas and prevent problems on the shoot day.

FASHION REFERENCES

At this point I would like to say I think it's incredibly important if you want to be a fashion or editorial makeup artist to have a very good pool of fashion image references already in your mind. I firmly believe you need to do your research in order to bring new and interesting makeup work to the table.

You won't be taken seriously as a fashion makeup artist if you don't know the major historical beauty looks of the 20th century. For example, you need to know what a Studio 54 eye is, what a Guy Bourdin woman looks like, or a 20's flapper mouth or an Edie Sedgwick makeup is. You can't be googling things on-set because you have no idea what people are talking about when they ask you for a specific makeup look or reference. You can't be expected to know everything but the more you do know the better, and you'll also enjoy the creative process more.

There are many great books and websites and YouTube channels so there is no lack of resources available. Be careful to avoid modern interpretations of vintage looks as they are often inaccurate – no one in the fashion industry wants to know what a seventeen-year-old YouTuber from Sweden thinks a 1920's flapper look is! Go to the original source, study it and then make your own interpretation of it.

Although you don't get asked every day for historical makeup, when you do you should be able to know and interpret the different makeup looks through history - which is why you need to educate yourself ahead of time on what the different periods of fashion are. It's also a necessity to keep educated about what is currently happening in the world of fashion – it's always evolving and changing. Although you never want to copy other people's work, you need to feed your eyes and your creativity by keeping up to date with the work being produced by the top photographers and stylists, and the aesthetic of the world's best magazines. Models.com is a great online resource to keep up with what is going on in the international fashion market, as well as the looking at the world's top creative representation agencies (like Streeters or Art Partner).

GETTING THE IMAGES FROM THE PHOTOGRAPHER

Getting the pictures from any type of shoot can sometimes take a while and might require some hassling (nicely!) on your part as photographers can get very busy and can find it hard to get the time to retouch the pictures or develop the film and scan it. Test shoots and go-see pictures in particular can take a long time to get back, as paid jobs might come in that need urgent retouching, pushing the test pictures to the back of the queue.

I think it's reasonable after a month to send a nice 'touching base' type email to the photographer and see if the images are nearly ready to be released. Then if not, every few weeks you could 'check in' to see if they're done. But be prepared, sometimes you will never get the pictures, especially when you're starting out. It does happen but as you progress and work with more established photographers, you will find this happens less and less. Naturally if a photographer never sends you the pictures, this is a great sign to move on and find different people to work with.

ORGANISING AND STORING YOUR IMAGES

Once the pictures are sent over to you by the photographer make sure you save them to your computer in an organised way that makes them easy to access later on. This makes them handy to find for future portfolio updates, and means you have a good record of the work that you have done. Ensure all your makeup photos are backed up either on an external hard drive that you keep off-site, or into the Cloud as you always want a backup if something happens to the originals.

This is what building a portfolio is all about. Once you have new images, you can update them onto your website and portfolio, and you can also post them to Instagram, which gives you a new opportunity to contact more photographers. As your portfolio improves so will the work opportunities that are available to you.

DO IT ALL AGAIN, BUT DO IT BETTER

Repeat this process until you have at least five stories that you are proud of that you can use for your initial portfolio/website and keep adding to them on a regular basis. Given that everyone reading this has very different life circumstances you'll have to decide how much time/energy you have to put into it. Just be patient and understanding that it is a process, for every makeup artist, not just you.

With all this broken down for you, you can see that shooting a whole portfolio is quite a daunting task. However, it doesn't have to be dozens and dozens of shoots to begin with – it's far better to have five or six really strong shoots with good photographers rather than many weaker shoots with a substandard group of photographers. Some of the initial shoots that you do may not be right to put in your portfolio (for different reasons), and that's fine and part of the process too.

Over time you will be replacing images in your portfolio with new work, and there will always be some timeless classics that you will want to keep. Some old favourites eventually will start to look out of date, so a portfolio is really constantly evolving.

A good tactic is to shoot things that you would like to get employed for in future. If you want to shoot swimwear campaigns, shoot a swimwear story. If you want to eventually shoot for a cosmetics brand, shoot beauty as if it was for a Rimmel ad campaign or for a skincare brand. It's harder to get booked on a particular type of job if it's not in your portfolio. Clients want to know that you have successfully done that type of work before, so it is important to shoot a range of work to put in your portfolio. It's also a good idea to have a mix of fashion and beauty.

When you are starting out, it can be difficult to engage people and get shoots organised, and many things can go wrong! Over the years, I've had some interesting days at work - the shoot where the photographer got quietly drunk over the course of the day (it turns out that his coffee cup didn't contain coffee), the shoot where we had to remove a dead peacock that had fallen out of a tree almost onto the model's head, the shoot where we nearly drowned at the beach as the tide came in and we had to carry all the clothes and equipment above our heads with chest high waves threatening to knock us over – I could go on! It's all a learning curve, so you need to be prepared for all eventualities.

FINDING YOUR STYLE

As you begin to build your portfolio and work with a variety of different photographers and teams, you will start to develop your own personal style of makeup. This is your secret sauce, and why you will end up getting booked on a job over other makeup artists. Some makeup artists are known for their bold use of colour, some for their glamorous and sophisticated evening makeup (see Charlotte Tilbury), some for their stripped back and more raw aesthetic.

It's up to you to find out what type of makeup that you love to do, which WILL come over time. By shooting and doing lots of different jobs on all different types of faces, you will figure out what type of makeup you want to do, and what type of makeup artist you want to be. It's not something that you can force into place or figure out intellectually – it's simply in the doing that it becomes clear. I know this probably sounds very abstract but like any artistic endeavour you do need to trust the process and allow your aesthetic to unfold by doing as much makeup as you possibly can.

The other way to hone this skill is to research all the best makeup artists that are currently producing the highest quality work in the world by looking at fashion magazines such as Vogue, Harper's Bazaar, Love, ELLE and i-D. By understanding the type of work that is being produced at the top levels of the industry, as well as historical fashion shoots, you feed your mind to improve your aesthetic and build up the reference pool you have in your head. This will give you ideas and enhance your creativity and allow you to experiment when you're shooting to push your work in different directions to see what works for you.

PORTFOLIO VS IPAD

Back in the old days your portfolio was a giant leather-bound book, and some photographers still tend to use leather bound book portfolios as it's a more impressive way to show their work. This is why your portfolio is sometimes called a 'book'. Filling your book involved literally tearing pages out of print magazines that your work had appeared in (hence why they are still sometimes called 'tear sheets') and putting them in your portfolio in a cohesive flow that best showcased the range of your makeup skills.

In the last few years, many creatives have now switched to using an iPad with a portfolio app which can then be taken to meetings and flicked through whilst speaking to the prospective client or creative. I use the Portfolio app for my portfolio on the iPad, and it works really well.

The beauty of using an iPad for your portfolio is it can be constantly updated with new digital images, and it can be the same as your website, so you only need to update one set of images. It saves a lot of time, and the other nice thing about the iPad is that it's easy to have different sections you can quickly turn on or off before a meeting with a particular client. You can show more commercial work to new potential commercial clients, and then switch on your cooler editorial for a meeting with a great new fashion magazine.

The other benefit of having an app like Portfolio on your iPad is that the images are stored on the iPad instead of the Cloud, so you aren't dependent on being able to connect to the Wi-Fi where you are showing your portfolio. It would crush your chances of getting a job if you couldn't show your book in a potential client meeting due to technical difficulties!

PUTTING YOUR PORTFOLIO IN ORDER

Figuring out the balance and the flow of your portfolio is an art form in itself, as you will be placing shoots that you have done next to each other, with a good progression to your overall book.

Think about it as if you're telling a story and giving an overall snapshot of your work - try and put images that complement each other in sequence and make it flow together well from one image to the next. The more shoots that you add to your book, the more skilled you will get at the portfolio process.

Overall your portfolio should show that you have good basic skills – you want to show some nice, natural makeup, beautiful clean skin, a lovely smoky eye, that you can do bright or dark lips perfectly, and perhaps some more interesting, conceptual makeup like a graphic eyeliner and a selection of editorial fashion makeup. Whatever else you want to put in there is up to you, but they are the very basics. If you do men's grooming or makeup for children's shoots, you should include those as well so that prospective clients know you have experience with them. It's also good to keep an eye on your overall portfolio being consistent, and not having too much variety in there, as it can look messy.

BASIC PORTFOLIO RULES

When I started my makeup career in Australia, I would periodically arrange to have a meeting with one of the bookers at the various Sydney creative agencies and they would give me feedback on my portfolio. (A booker is the person at a creative agency who organises an artist's schedule of jobs and handles their administration/career details.) Some of the things I learnt generally about structuring a portfolio:

- Have a strong opener image. This might be the only one they remember and needs to represent you as a whole. I think the best way to choose this picture is to think of what work you have done best represents your æsthetic and style of makeup. You should love it and feel proud when you see it and think it expresses the essence of what you do best.
- Have a strong image to finish.
- Generally, it's best to have your more recent work at the beginning, but if your portfolio is well edited enough it doesn't need to be in the order of when you shot it.
- Be ruthless. An image is only as good as the weakest link so if the clothes or hair are dated, or the model isn't great or their pose is cheesy, it doesn't matter how good the picture is, what it was published in or how technically brilliant the makeup is, it needs to go.
- It's good to start off with more natural work and flow into stronger makeup to show you can do a strong lip, a good smoky eye, more difficult technical makeup as well as beautiful natural skin, lovely eyeliner and so on. The opener should still be strong-ish though, showing a variety of technical skills.
- Make sure your portfolio shows you can do all sorts of makeup, but always within your style. Care needs to be taken with this as it's very important that it all looks like YOUR work (this goes back to the development of your style that will come about over time.)

- Ensure you have a good representation of all ethnicities in your book – you want to show that you can do a full range of skin tones.
- If you don't want to get booked for a certain type of shoot, don't put it in your portfolio. If you hate shooting swimwear models on the beach, don't put it in your book. If you don't like working with children, don't put them in your book. This sounds like such simple common sense but one of the artists that I assisted at the beginning told me that, and it was great advice. You can get all excited about the latest story that you shot but if it's not the type of work you want more of, don't put it in. Likewise if you want to be a fashion makeup artist, don't put shoots with glamour models in your book.
- If you have a lot of beauty images, or do a lot of celebrity or male grooming, it can be worth having separate books for each of those things on your online portfolio. I have a Women's Book, a Men's Book, an Advertising Book and a Beauty Book at present, with a Celebrity Book on the way. It allows clients to focus in on specific types of your work that they need to see without having a single enormous portfolio to go through.
- If you don't have enough images to create separate books for kids/men/beauty, put them together so you have a mini section for each within your book.
- Try not to use more than four images from a shoot especially where the makeup is the same.
- Keep it short but sweet, especially when you're starting. It's better to have less images that are all strong than many more weak images.

If you can get feedback from an agency or another creative, like a photographer or hairdresser you work with regularly, a fresh set of eyes can be invaluable to see what's working and what's not. Sometimes pictures we happen to love aren't selling our work as much as we'd like. You may get different advice from different people and you'll learn to filter what is right for you.

CHAPTER 4

How to Build Your Website

Your website is your shop window to the world, so take some time constructing it. I often get asked what's the best way to do this, and whether people need to hire someone to do it for them, as this can get really expensive.

Feel free to hire someone, but my honest advice would be to use a site like Wix.com (which is free) or Squarespace.com, which is pretty inexpensive. Both are easy to use and the templates look good. Your website doesn't have to be super fancy, it just needs to communicate your work to your prospective clients, so the quicker and more cheaply you can get a decent website up and running the better. If you find you are getting stuck whilst you are putting it together, YouTube has thousands of videos on almost any aspect of the process that can help you out, plus they have good customer support at both Wix and Squarespace to help you if you need it.

GETTING STARTED

As a starting point, look to see what other people in the industry are doing. Research is key in any industry, so I would suggest you use Instagram and find other artists where you live, then go to their websites and see how they structure their website, where they put their client lists, what other details they include about themselves, and what sections they have in their portfolio.

Then think about your own site and what elements you think you should include about yourself - how you might structure your biography and CV and client list and lay out your site. Look at what you like and what makes sense. Prospective clients don't want to spend hours looking at your website or having to click through loads of screens to find what they want about you. It needs to be a snapshot of your work. Remember it's a short ad, not a film! Your website needs to have just as much care put into it as your portfolio.

Then simply put up the images that you currently have and build from there. Your website is also a place to keep a list of your clients and the magazine titles that you have worked for, and a bio if you wish to include one so people can learn more about you. Naturally at the beginning you won't have much, but that's fine. If I had one mantra for being a makeup artist it would be: 'Do what you can, with what you have now." The hardest bit is always the beginning so it's a matter of pushing through that, and as long as you're getting better and doing the work, you will progress.

Also having a site you can maintain yourself means that you don't run the risk of the person who created it for you quitting their business leaving you with no idea about how to update your website, and stuck finding someone else who can do it for you. I know a number of creatives that this has happened to, so don't let this happen to you. It's essential to have a website that you can update quickly and easily. It also means you don't have to wait for your web manager to be available if you need to update or tweak something quickly. The other option is that you could pay someone to set it up for you and then maintain it yourself, but make sure you know how to keep it updated on your own.

The other things that are super important to clearly put on your website are your email address and mobile number, as well as your social media handles. Make them clearly visible and as easy as possible for people to find you, and the more options they have to contact you, the better. I know this probably seems incredibly obvious, but you would be amazed how many people don't do it. Check your messages regularly and be as contactable as possible.

Be careful if you're using an email contact form on your website – you need to confirm periodically that it's still working, and also scan your junk or spam email folder occasionally to make sure important work emails aren't ending up there.

Make sure that your website works across all devices as well, bearing in mind that many people will be looking at your website on their mobile phone.

VIDEO AND MOVING IMAGE

It can also be an option to have a moving image section on your website these days, to show that you can comfortably and confidently do video work. As it's a medium that's increasingly being used, it's good to show that you can do it as well – makeup can behave differently on moving image/film. (Note - moving image work is sometimes also known as your 'showreel'.)

DO I NEED A WEBSITE IF I HAVE INSTAGRAM?

The short answer to this is yes. Some creatives that are newer to the industry say they can get away with just having an up to date Instagram, (and yes, your Instagram should be up to date), but I advise against just having Instagram. A website is a necessity to look professional and to showcase your work, even if many people might check your Instagram first.

Having a good website is one of the key parts of your marketing strategy/approach. Think of your website as a summary of your best work, which allows you to demonstrate the breadth of your work and a full complement of your abilities, and Instagram is what you are up to right now to show a little more personality. Of course, you need to be careful what sort of personality you're showing on Instagram but that's part of a bigger conversation that we will get to in the next chapter.

CHAPTER 5

Social Media

So your website is finished, your portfolio is gradually building up, and you want to get maximum value out of the work that you have done. The next stage is using your images to market your work. This is where a judicious use of social media comes in.

INSTAGRAM

Instagram has been a game changer over the last few years. It's a visual medium, thus perfect for demonstrating what fashion creatives are doing and as a result, many of the old ways of showing your work are a lot less effective now. Instagram is the ultimate social media tool to showcase your makeup.

Obviously this could change anytime as another platform could become more important – now TikTok is the fastest growing social media platform, and only you can decide if that's something you want to try out in future. Given the recent success of some makeup artists on TikTok I think this is one of the most interesting areas of social media to potentially explore.

But for the moment, for promoting yourself in fashion, I believe Instagram is where you should focus most of your marketing efforts.

This is where your audience is — many people in the fashion industry turn to Instagram now when they are looking for new talent to book on a job. It's also an incredible research tool, allowing you to find and connect with all the people that will help you to make your new career a reality.

The beauty of Instagram is you can use it as much as you like, and it's free apart from the time you put into it. That's the trick of it — because it is possible to put infinite amounts of time into it without seeing many results. Thus, you want to put some effort into it each day but figure out what works and what doesn't work for you in terms of increasing your followers, and the response that you get to each post. Building an Instagram following is hard and time consuming, but if you are patient and do some each day your audience will gradually build up.

INSTAGRAM TIPS

- It's a good idea to have a separate work and private Instagram if you want to put up personal things on Instagram. It's alright to put a bit of personal stuff on your work Instagram - people do love a good selfie! But you don't want to have dozens of pictures of your kids or you eating lunch all the time with friends, otherwise it detracts from your actual makeup work. Make it easy for prospective clients to see your makeup work, as if they have to wade through quite a few non-makeup related posts to get to your makeup posts, it's probably not giving the effect you want. More personal posts can also go on Instagram Stories, but more on that later.
- Also make it easy for people to FIND you on Instagram — I think it's best to have your name as your Instagram username or something simple and makeup or beauty related that people can remember. If your name is already taken on Instagram or more common than

other names, you could always choose something like '@clairesmithbeauty or @clairesmithmakeup'. Using your childhood nickname as your Insta handle is not going to make it painless for prospective clients to find you.

- Be sure to include your website and any other contact details in your Instagram profile to make it as easy as possible to get hold of you. It can be useful to have your email in your Instagram profile as some prospective clients might prefer to send you an email than an Instagram direct message. The more ways you have to be quickly contacted, the better. Include your city where you work as well, which helps take the guesswork out of where in the world you are if a client is thinking of hiring you for something.

- It's a good idea to have a think about what type of posts you want to post on your Instagram account so you can build a cohesive feed. Naturally you will be posting your makeup work, but you also might want to post occasional pictures of makeup products, or How-To videos, or maybe you take beautiful scenic location pictures. This means you don't have to have a constant avalanche of new editorial work all the time to keep your feed updated, and also helps your profile stand out from other makeup artists in your area. Just make sure that the bulk of your feed is still your makeup work though, so it's clear that you are a working makeup artist and people can easily find your current work on your Instagram.

It can take a while to get an idea of the best flow of your feed, so experiment with it whilst you don't have too many followers. The most important thing is to post as regularly as you can, in order to get the Instagram algorithm working in your favour. It's also better to keep what you post high-quality, so if you feel like you only have two good images a week, make that your posting schedule.

BUILDING COMMUNITY

It's also really important to engage with other Instagram users to grow your account and build a community of supporters for your work. You do this by following accounts that you think might also like your work, and by liking their posts and being present on their accounts, and slowly you will build up your followers. The people who follow you are into what you do, and you should treat them well, recognising that they are supportive of your work and you in turn can then be supportive of theirs.

My best advice is to spend some time testing out different types of accounts to follow – you could try other makeup artists, stylists, photographers, model agencies, manicurists, magazines, beauty brands... the lists of accounts to try is literally endless. Over time you will find certain types of accounts are more likely to follow you back, so it's about testing out what works and what doesn't to increase your following.

Being present on social media to the people that you would like to work with and building on your local network of clients and peers in the industry will keep you top of mind for when a job comes up. Leave comments and engage with what other people are posting, and over time people will reciprocate. Of course it's important to focus mainly on the local market that you are in, but what's amazing about social media is that it's possible to build an online community of supporters, world-wide.

I know it seems like a lot of work (and it is!) to build an Instagram account from scratch, but I have personally found it to be an invaluable tool. You are trying to attract a difficult market – fashion photographers/stylists/fashion clients and other creatives must be amongst some of the hardest people in the world to engage and attract. So, it's up to you to be persistent, keep producing the best makeup you can and then SHOW YOUR DAMN WORK. Instagram is where they are going to find you at present, and it makes sense to invest effort into it.

Newsflash – no one apart from your mum and dad, your partner and maybe your Auntie Doris really care that you are now doing makeup. It's not because people are horrible, but everyone, including you, is occupied with the details of their own lives. As my friend and mentor, makeup artist Kay Montano, says, 'The world has never needed another makeup artist'.

This shouldn't be disheartening – just because the world doesn't need another makeup artist doesn't mean you can't create a good space for yourself doing the work you love. But what it does mean is that you have to carve that space out for yourself. No one else is going to do the work for you, and no one else is going to care as passionately about your work as you do. It's up to you to show your work to the right audiences who will be interested. So, you can't be discouraged at the beginning when you post and post and post... and crickets chirp. Tumbleweeds roll. You keep posting into outer space... and still nothing. This is normal, and it happened to me too, but I've put in a lot of time and effort and now my Instagram account when I was writing this book is over 13k followers. If you keep going, people will start to respond.

This is the double-edged sword of Instagram – it does work to get people's attention, but it also demands a LOT of time. Don't forget that Instagram is not there as a warm and fuzzy gift from Mark Zuckerberg to you – he wants your attention and lots of it in exchange for using the platform. Thus, I would encourage you to be strict about how long you spend on the platform each day and set time limits for yourself as the other thing about it, which isn't news to anyone, is it's highly addictive.

My best advice for Instagram is to have a plan of how long you'll spend on it each day, how many people you want to follow or leave comments on, and use a timer if necessary, to remind you not to hang around on Instagram too long. Do the work each day and then get off Instagram. Go back to your life and work out, see some friends, read a book, clean your brushes, tidy your kit, play with your dog (especially play with your dog!) – do whatever is the stuff of your real, off-line life. Being consistent about daily Instagram work, working your plan and giving it some time will allow your Instagram strategy to work. Will it happen in days? No. Months? Maybe. Years? Yes.

Becoming a makeup artist takes time and you need patience to give your work time to flourish. Instagram is part of this long-term strategy and needs to be managed the same way. Then eventually you will start to see your followers increasing, and people will start to contact you for work based on what they've seen on your Instagram.

USING INSTAGRAM

Instagram Stories

This is definitely worth looking into as part of your Instagram strategy, since as of 2021, half a billion people globally use Instagram Stories every day. It doesn't take long to learn - you can figure it out by playing around with it yourself, or by watching a couple of YouTube tutorials and just experiment with different ways of using it. There is an art to great Instagram Stories, and some people are definitely better at it than others. Like everything on your Instagram plan it's worth having a try and finding out what works best for you.

The beauty of Instagram Stories is that it disappears in 24 hours (with an option to keep them) so the content can be more disposable and can be a nice window into your real-life world so people can get to know more about you and what you're up to. Of course, it's fine if you don't like posting on Instagram Stories, just focus on what you like to post on your Instagram feed and what you feel is resonating with your audience.

Instagram Reels

Instagram's newest feature, Reels, launched in 2020 and is a direct competitor to TikTok. Reels is designed to have easy-to-use technology to create videos – they can be recorded all at once, or as a series of clips, or you can upload photos from your existing photo library. There are tools to play with the speed, add audio effects or add special effects. Reels is quite an interesting option for makeup artists as it's another medium to show your makeup work, on the main platform where your audience already is. It will be interesting to see if Reels takes off in the same way that Instagram Stories did a couple of years ago.

Instagram TV

This is fairly new but also potentially interesting as its use is growing very quickly also, and it can be an excellent way to show the type of makeup that you do. @nikkimakeup did a great job of really growing her career via doing weekly tutorials on Instagram TV.

A FINAL NOTE ON INSTAGRAM

Don't get discouraged because you can see other makeup artists with literally a million followers, and you're stuck under 1,000. Apparently the first 1,000 followers are the hardest to attain, and once you crack that barrier it gets easier. Don't worry about what other people are doing – you concentrate on doing you, as best you can. Even taking ten minutes to post a picture whilst you have a coffee can pay dividends over time to keep your audience engaged.

Also take into account that many, many people on Instagram have either bought followers or use software to build their account, so big Instagram numbers can be deceiving. I don't advocate using fake followers for a number of reasons, although I know it's tempting if you see other people with loads of followers and you're there spending hours and hours bashing away trying to get above a few hundred. The reason I don't recommend using software or fake followers to build your account is:

- Instagram are cracking down on those accounts which means if your followers are fake, half of them can be wiped out in a day.
- You aren't building community by doing this and your engagement on your pictures will be low which isn't what you want.

And finally, if you are so busy with your makeup work that you don't have much time for Instagram, that's a great problem to have! Have an Instagram presence, but if you have so much work that you worry about maintaining it, I would argue that Instagram is not super important for you at this stage of your career. I know some photographers who are inundated with work and worry they don't put enough effort into Instagram – but Instagram is supposed to be there to promote your work so it's a good problem to have to be too busy for it.

OTHER SOCIAL MEDIA PLATFORMS

Another question I hear a lot is do I need to be on other platforms like YouTube, or Facebook, or Twitter or LinkedIn or TikTok? The most important thing to consider when answering this is it depends on what type of brand you wish to build for your makeup career. Each type of social media has a different audience, and some platforms will work better for the type of makeup you do than others.

My answer to this is please feel free to test out any of these platforms as they might be great for you, but I don't believe they are a necessity for fashion makeup success. As long as you're on Instagram, as of 2021, that is where your audience is which is why I believe it should be your main focus. Feel free to experiment with other platforms but I've tried a few of them and they have never really brought me anything.

It's also very time consuming and brain draining being on multiple social media platforms, and although you can definitely build audiences on all of them, you need to decide how much energy and focus you have to put into each one. I would suggest that organising the shoots to build your portfolio is already very time consuming and you'll need to decide where your best marketing efforts should be put. However, depending on what type of work you want to do, other social media platforms might be worth exploring.

Facebook

I think Facebook is great if you want to book more private clients and brides. If this is your focus, I would strongly advise looking into Facebook ads and building a good presence there.

Other ways that Facebook can be useful is for Creative Pages and Groups – there are various pages that are essentially message boards for creatives seeking other members of a shoot team to get a test/submission off the ground. There are also sometimes paid jobs on there, so certainly at the beginning of your career they can be an excellent conduit to potential work. For instance, the page 'London Hair & Makeup Artists' has 10k followers, and there are plenty of smaller pages like it on Facebook as well. Once you are working, you can ask different members of your network if they know of any Facebook groups also. There are also private WhatsApp groups in different cities that share jobs, and this can be something useful to discuss with other hair and makeup people in your network once that starts to grow.

As I mentioned before with keeping separate private and professional Instagram accounts, I think this also holds true for Facebook and Twitter. It's very easy to share posts across different social media channels so once you have it all set up it should be quite quick and easy to keep your makeup social media updated.

Twitter

I used to be a big Twitter user a few years ago and found it very useful to promote myself when I had a makeup blog, but not many fashion creatives I know really use it now. Feel free to experiment with this but I never found it helped me get more makeup work.

LinkedIn

This is handy to have a page on as sometimes businesses who might want to hire you like to check your LinkedIn profile, but I wouldn't put too much time into it. If you have a LinkedIn page, just make sure it's up to date.

YouTube

This could be an interesting platform if you wanted to promote your makeup work via makeup tutorials. Doing the tutorials can be time consuming but might be worth exploring if you like being on camera and enjoy doing them. It's not something that ever appealed to me personally, but it's definitely potentially an interesting option to help build your career – Lisa Eldridge has managed to very successfully combine being a YouTuber and an editorial makeup artist and leveraged both careers simultaneously. YouTube can also be good if you have a lot of video work – music videos, advertising etc. It's quite easy to embed a file and you can create a channel to display your video work.

Snapchat

If you're on Snapchat that's great, but it's not a platform that I have used to get jobs (there are only so many hours in a day and I don't have time to do more social media than I am already doing!) I don't know many people who use it in fashion to market their work.

TikTok

Again, this might be an interesting platform depending on the type of makeup work that you do. TikTok is predicted by the analytics firm App Annie to reach 1.2 billion monthly active users in 2021, so it has the power to potentially be a great way to build your audience. It also has a different demographic to the other social media platforms, so you could reach a huge amount of new viewers, mainly Generation Z. The only way to know for sure is to try the different social media platforms out and see if they work for you to build the type of career that you want.

SECTION TWO

Getting out there

So, let's say that you have just finished makeup college, you know the areas of makeup you want to work in, and you're all excited about your newfound abilities, but really not sure about how to get the ball on your brand new career rolling.

What to do next? There are a couple of options to start getting your name out into the industry and focusing on increasing the necessary skills that you need in order to eventually get those big, exciting jobs that you'd love to do.

FOCUS ON BUILDING YOUR PORTFOLIO

You can just get started and focus on building your portfolio as quickly as possible (using the method described in Chapter 2) as after all, every job that you do builds your confidence, your experience and your knowledge of what's required. Or, and this was my preferred method, you could start assisting more established makeup artists.

Also bear in mind it doesn't have to be one path or the other – you could start to contact people for assisting work, and at the same time build your portfolio and your network alongside your assisting work. I think you're probably starting to understand that the time frame on both building your portfolio AND getting assisting work coming in is fairly long, so doing both simultaneously is I think, a good idea.

CHAPTER 6

Assisting

This was how I got started in high fashion makeup. Basically, it means contacting established makeup artists already working in the industry and helping them with whatever they need to do their job. In exchange you learn how great makeup artists work on the technical side, discover what the day to day reality of being a makeup artist is like, and begin to network with other assistants who are at your level within the industry. Some of the greatest fashion teams in the world all met whilst they were assisting. Top photographer David Sims started working with the hairstylist Guido when they were both assisting in London in the 90's. And they still work together today!

Assisting allows you to be exposed to work at much higher levels of the industry that might take years to get to, if you ever do. Through assisting, I have been able to work on most of the global major magazine titles such as Vogue, i-D, Harper's Bazaar, ELLE, Numero, Pop and Vanity Fair amongst many others. You get to work on bigger productions and learn makeup techniques from really amazing established artists. Years of assisting made me feel confident that I knew what to expect on pretty much any job whether it's a celebrity, a cover, a beauty story or an ad campaign because I have experienced working with some of the world's best makeup artists at the peak of their careers.

Sounds good? There is a catch. It's incredibly competitive to get into and it pays very little money. Much of your assisting work will be for free, especially at the beginning, to give you experience. It's often assisting on editorial days that the makeup artist needs extra help with, like a big beauty shoot. Sometimes if it's an advertising job you will get paid, but generally that's for the more experienced makeup assistants who have been doing makeup for a while.

Music videos or TV commercials often use assistants as there can be numbers of back up dancers/singers and extra talent to make up, and that might be paid or unpaid, depending on your experience level and whether you've worked with that artist before.

Just as an FYI - unless you work full-time for an artist as an assistant it can be difficult to earn enough to live on just being an assistant, but if you can juggle it with other makeup or part-time work, the experience you get can be invaluable.

WHAT SKILLS YOU NEED FOR ASSISTING

Every artist is different and what they want from an assistant is different. Sometimes you will be doing makeup on talent/models on your own, or sometimes you might be helping to keep the artist organised, cleaning their station and setting up their kit as well as getting them tea/coffee and anything else they might need whilst they work.

Chances are pretty good you will be washing brushes, but you might also be arranging products from PRs to be sent to the studio, running out to get baby wipes or tissues or eyelash glue, doing nails, doing body makeup, doing male talent or background people, doing fake tans and mini facials or watching the shot when the main artist is busy working on another model. For very high-level makeup artists it can also involve PA work, such as sorting out bills, banking, administration – things the main artist finds hard to do when they're working constantly.

One of the most important things is that the main makeup artist wants to be around you for a whole day at work. Shooting back to back all the time can get lonely, and it's physically demanding and mentally draining, so makeup artists want assistants that they like who can help them have the best day at work possible. Having the right attitude is absolutely invaluable and is what will get you booked (and re-booked) to assist an artist rather than someone else. Being positive and cheerful with a 'can do' attitude is ideal.

HOW TO BE A GREAT ASSISTANT

Always get to work early, pay attention to what they might need next, make sure they have enough to drink and their lunch is organised the way they like it. Your job is to take the pressure off the main artist as much as you can. No one expects you to have Pat McGrath-level makeup skills, and the level of makeup skill that you need depends on the level at which you are assisting. Thus, when you're starting out and have no assisting experience, think about asking newer, less established artists if you can assist them (for free) on a smaller job. Then like everything, you build from there.

Even when you're assisting, treat every job with as much pride as if it were your own. Of course, don't be weird about it, it's still the work of the artist you are assisting as they are responsible for the makeup on that job overall, but don't ever think 'oh it's just body makeup' or 'it's just the background dancers' or 'it's not my gig, it doesn't matter'. It DOES matter. Don't forget that the person that you are assisting is responsible for your work and how you perform and behave on-set, so you want to make sure you reflect well on them at all times.

Key Skills:

- Learn how they like to work as quickly as you can and get a feel for how they like their kit arranged.

- ○ Keep an eye on what's going on without hovering too much, nobody likes someone lurking like a serial killer in the background.
- ○ Don't ask makeup questions whilst they are doing makeup, or touch their products whilst they are working, let them concentrate.
- ○ Try and anticipate what they might need.
- ○ Don't talk on set (I know some of the big photographers or makeup artists who don't let their assistants talk AT ALL unless someone speaks to them first, but I think that's a bit excessive.)
- ○ Be polite and friendly and just chip in if something needs doing.
- ○ It's better to be quiet than loud and for the love of god don't give opinions about any aspect of the shoot. No one wants to hear if you don't like the hair extensions or the red dress might be better.

So just BE NICE. Don't behave in a way that you wouldn't want someone else to behave to you. Don't gossip. Naturally I don't have to tell you to look neat and clean and have a kit to match. Don't sit down if the artist is standing, and no mobile phone use whilst working unless you ask first. For instance, if you have to make an urgent personal call or answer an email at lunchtime, ask first. No one wants you buried in your phone when you're needed. Yes, watching the shot to wait to re-powder can be boring. No, that doesn't mean it's time to catch up with your friends on WhatsApp or look at Instagram.

No social media of anything unless you've been told it's alright explicitly by who you are assisting. If it's a celebrity no selfies, no staring, no generally being weird. It's not about you when you're assisting, so do whatever is needed with a minimum of fuss. And keep your personal life at home – telling the whole crew you had a fight with your boyfriend that morning is the fast track to not getting rebooked.

Nothing should be too big or too small a task for you – it's all part of the job. Do everything with a smile. All of it is great experience for your future makeup career and allows you to build on your knowledge and increase your network.

BENEFITS OF ASSISTING

Learning

Obviously there are all the makeup tips, tricks and techniques you will learn as every artist has a different skill set and different way of working. This alone is invaluable and can take years off your development time as an artist. But the other most valuable aspect of assisting is how to be on-set.

It teaches you the politics and dynamics of different photo teams, how to do makeup for different lighting set ups, when you should go in to re-powder or touch up, and when you shouldn't, and how to deal with tricky clients or how to manage different opinions and juggle difficult circumstances when there are a publicists and celebrities and managers and brands and art directors all with their own agenda. Learning how to behave on a day like that is going to be one of the greatest things you learn from your time as an assistant.

Networking with Other Assistants

The other major advantage to assisting is the networking opportunities it gives you. If there is an appropriate moment in the day and you can quietly get a chance to speak to the other assistants (assistant photographer, stylist, hairdresser) then it's fine for you to network with them and in fact this is a wonderful way to broaden your contacts. Just make sure you do it discreetly and don't let the networking aspect impinge on your ability to do your job. Needless to say, be respectful to the artist that you're assisting and make sure you don't try and network with the other senior people on set, such as the client, photographer or art director. You definitely won't get rebooked if the artist thinks you are after their work.

This amazingly does happen sometimes, as some assistants will try to poach a client or photographer which is pretty much the worst thing you can do and won't be forgotten anytime soon. People in fashion have loooooong memories. I can think of a few people who have bad reputations still from doing things like this in the 1990's, so don't forget everyone you meet you will probably be seeing around the traps for many years to come, thus treat everyone well.

HOW DO I GET ASSISTING WORK?

There are two main ways to get assisting work – through agencies, and through artists. I've personally always used agencies to get assisting work, but the second way which is now a very viable option, is contacting artists directly and asking to assist them. You can do this either through Instagram or email.

The good news is, once you have proven yourself to an agency or an artist, you can get more work. And once you have assisted a couple of established artists, it's easier to get more assisting work.

GETTING ASSISTING WORK THROUGH AN AGENCY

First off, you need to research the creative agencies in your area. As mentioned previously, most cities have a number of creative agencies that look after and manage makeup artists, hairdressers, stylists, manicurists and photographers. They need a pool of good assistants they can call on to help out their artists on different jobs. You want to be on that list, and over time as you keep working for that agency and assisting different artists, you will work your way up the list and hopefully, get good, regular work.

You need to know who their artists are and understand the type of makeup they do – is their roster of artists more commercial or more high fashion? What magazine titles do their artists shoot for? What celebrity clients do they have?

My best tip is to look for the more junior people the agency represents and ask to assist them. The agency will usually start you with one of their most junior artists anyway, so the agency can test you out. Don't ask to assist someone like Lucia Pica the first time you contact them – it's not going to happen if the agency don't already know you and trust that you will be reliable and do a great job.

I asked Emma Davies from The Emma Davies Agency in London what her best advice was for getting noticed when you are first contacting agencies for assisting work. She says you should contact every agency and makeup artist you can find, and let them know that you're available, you're happy to do anything needed and be willing to work for free. Be friendly and polite in your email and have a good knowledge of the artists at that particular agency.

You are seeking to build a relationship with an agency, so be honest, trustworthy and persistent without being annoying and over time, you will start to get to know some of them and they will likely give you a try. Emma also had a tip for building agency relationships – "If it's appropriate, ask an agent for their advice on what you could do next or do better. Everyone likes to be helpful and not only do you get invaluable feedback about next steps in your career, it's a great way of building rapport with someone."

As you continue to assist at the agency and they get to know you better, eventually you might be booked for their overflow work. This is work that either none of the makeup artists at the agency is available for, or that isn't the right level for their artists to take on. It could involve doing the skin on a male grooming job for a top hairdresser (I used to do quite a lot of those jobs when I was assisting), or a more minor celebrity for a red-carpet job, or body or hand makeup for a still life shoot. It allows them to fulfil a client request without having one of their main artists booked for a whole day on a smaller job.

When I used to assist at D+V Management I was getting some great work in this way, doing Burberry and Lanvin Men campaigns and being asked to do male grooming for celebrities for US Vogue, but I'd been with the agency for about three years by that point. I had assisted almost every single one of their artists and hairdressers at least once, so D+V knew me well.

Assisting at an agency also gives you potential access to working with all their artists if they like you, not just one. It's very competitive to get assisting slots, and it is worth reaching out to all the creative agencies in your city. Spread your net far and wide and see what comes back.

Lastly if you are assisting for an agency, they will ask for feedback from the artist about whether they liked you or not. Based on this feedback, the agency will (or won't) use you again.

GETTING ASSISTING WORK DIRECTLY THROUGH AN ARTIST

The second way to get assisting work is to contact the artist directly. Just follow makeup artists on Instagram and after a period of time if you like the type of work they do, send them a direct message or email and ask to assist them. You might get an answer, or you may not, but just keep liking their work and be persistent.

Being tenacious in your pursuit of what you want, without being annoying, is a huge part of becoming a makeup artist. I always have people messaging me on Instagram asking to assist me, and even though I have a regular team of assistants I work with, it's the people that constantly stay visible, liking and commenting on my feed that I remember a few months later when I need someone new. 99% of people send one message and then disappear, never to be seen again. Don't be in that 99%! Send your messages, be respectful yet visible and don't get discouraged. You will get a break at some point.

Again, I would start by contacting newer artists on Instagram who do great work but have less followers rather than someone with a million followers or a major celebrity makeup artist. There are so many brilliant makeup artists who do amazing makeup that you can find on Instagram, who might need a new assistant.

Another great tip for getting assisting work is offering to help clean, organise and perhaps help downsize their makeup kit, especially if you're skilled at organising. Or if you're good at social media, offer to help the artist look after that. Or offer to help out with admin tasks like managing PR credits (more on that later) if they need help with that side of things.

I guarantee that every working makeup artist has a bunch of things they don't have time to do that you could help them with, you just need to make suggestions of what you could do to jog their memories. I always have way too much to do for the number of hours in the day, and now my amazing assistants help me with the things I can't get to because I'm busy shooting. Once a makeup artist gets a chance to see how great you are, you'll get asked back.

HOW TO SEND THE RIGHT EMAIL TO AN AGENCY

To contact the agency, send the agency an email – you are one of many people contacting the agency at that point, but there are a few things you can do to make your email stand out.

First things first – make sure your email has good punctuation and spelling. These things really matter. I personally would be far less likely to take on an assistant who hadn't taken the time to craft a decently written, correctly spelled email or message. Don't bombard them with attachments, but it's a good idea to include a PDF of your latest work on the email, and your CV as well. Make sure you include a (working!) link to your Instagram, website and up to date email address and phone numbers.

Make sure that your contact details are easy to find on the email - you would be surprised how hard it is to find some people's mobile numbers, which means no job for them when something comes in last moment. Say you are happy to work for free in order to help the artist and that no job is too big or too small for you. Making coffee, washing brushes, cleaning their kit – these are all things you'd be happy to do.

You may not get an answer, and that's OK. I would keep working on your portfolio, and sometime later (perhaps a couple of months), touch base with the agency or artist again, show your new work and say you're still keen to assist. If you keep doing this in a polite way, without spamming them, eventually you might be added to their agency assisting list.

Also follow the agency on Instagram, and the artist you want to assist, and like the work they are posting. Be around where they can see you! Do this consistently – it can take months for people to even vaguely know who you are, so you can't send one Instagram 'Like' and think that that is sufficient to get you booked on a job.

WHAT TO HAVE IN AN ASSISTING MAKEUP KIT

You don't usually need your full makeup kit when you're assisting, but it's a good idea to have the basics ready to go in case you get a last minute assisting job. This should include:

- Set bag
- Brushes
- Brush cleanser
- Skincare
- Body products (moisturiser, body makeup)
- Powder (for all skin tones)
- Extra tissues, wipes and cotton buds
- Basic nail kit
- Basic male grooming kit

Always ask the artist you're assisting or their booker at their agency what they would like you to bring in case they want you to have something in particular. Once you start contacting agencies/artists to assist, you need to be ready to work at short notice with any type of kit from a small one to a full kit with everything in it (glitter, lashes, body paints etc.).

Sometimes the artist you are assisting will want you with your full kit, sometimes you will work out of the artist's kit, but when I was assisting I always liked to have a bit of my own makeup (including my brushes) so that I had my own products handy if I needed them. Just a small carry-on suitcase or bag is generally fine. Quicker than rummaging through another makeup artist's kit as well in an on-set emergency - they do happen! It's also a good idea to discreetly familiarise yourself as quickly as you can with an artist's kit when you first start assisting them, so you know where things are and how they like things organised.

HIGH LEVEL ASSISTING

Very established and successful fashion makeup artists like Val Garland will have a team of assistants. Their main assistant who is usually on every job with them is called the First Assistant, and the typical time for a First Assistant to stay with one artist before heading off to work on their own is about three to five years, although some people stay longer than that. There will also be a Second Assistant and sometimes a Third as well, depending on how busy the main makeup artist is.

If the First Assistant works full-time for the artist, he or she will generally get a small monthly salary, usually about minimum wage, to pay for them to live whilst they work. At that level - I'm talking about the highest level, such as Peter Philips or Diane Kendal – historically you would be flying around the world and working a lot so it can be very difficult to have a personal life or a family if you're constantly on a plane. But obviously if the opportunity arises and you want to go for it, it's an incredible experience as the contacts you make have the capacity to help launch you to the highest levels of fashion when you're finished with assisting.

Just a note – you will need to be really quite experienced as a makeup artist before you would be considered to assist a major international makeup artist. However, if this is what you want, my advice is to get some initial assisting experience by assisting some more junior artists, as well as working on your portfolio. Then after you are pretty proficient both as a makeup artist and as an assistant, get in contact with bigger international makeup artists via their agency.

DO I NEED TO ASSIST?

I'm a huge fan of assisting and think every makeup artist can benefit from doing at least a bit of it. However, it's definitely not a necessity and Instagram and the internet has opened up a ton of opportunities that mean the days of doing years of assisting in order to develop your career are no longer one of the only options available to get ahead. There are many very successful and internationally renowned makeup artists who have never assisted anyone (Pat McGrath, Isamaya Ffrench and Mary Greenwell, to name a few) so it's certainly not a prerequisite to having a great career. If you want to just jump in and get started building your book and contacting clients, go for it.

KNOW YOUR HISTORY

Finally, before you start assisting, begin to teach yourself about who is working in fashion. You need to understand who the major creatives in fashion photography have been in the last 20-70 years. It's inexcusable to be working in fashion and not know who Mario Sorrenti is, or Peter Philips, or Sam McKnight or Joe McKenna. This is all part of becoming a fashion makeup artist - learning what has come before, and who the work was created by.

It's never been easier to research anything with the internet now, so there are no excuses for not knowing the basics of the history of fashion. No-one expects you to know everything but having a good idea of who the major photographers, stylists, hairdressers and makeup artists of the last few decades are is a great starting point and will help you to stand out from the other assistants.

CHAPTER 7

Relationships and Networking

I can't begin to tell you how important this is, your network is EVERYTHING. If you haven't been using the power of your network, then you have some seriously good things that are about to come your way by using it in a systematic and organised way.

I would say honestly that almost all the good things that came into my career came from my network. When you think about it, it's logical. People need to know you exist before they can hire you. And how do they know about that? From the people who already know you, who have worked with you before and would (and do!) recommend you.

Networking has a pretty bad reputation – the word alone makes you think of sleazy salesmen in cheap suits handing out business cards at conventions and wheeling and dealing. Networking is quite simply fostering relationships that are mutually beneficial.

I consider your network any of the creatives you have worked with – clients, designers, photographers, stylists, hairdressers, manicurists, producers, set designers, choreographers, casting directors, videographers and directors. And if you haven't done any jobs yet, and you feel you don't have any network at all, don't panic!

HOW TO BUILD YOUR NETWORK

I think Instagram is the quickest and easiest way to build your network in whichever area you choose to work, whether it be fashion, bridal, television or so on.

Simply start with one person you know, and then click through who they work with and work your way out from there. If you don't know where to start, try going through the Instagram of magazines that you like and find who is shooting for them (hint – focus on smaller, independent magazines that are being produced in your city to start off with.) Of course, just because you've found someone on Instagram doesn't mean you will contact them, but by doing some thorough research you'll begin to put together a picture of the fashion community in your area. Build a presence by following them, and liking and commenting on their posts so you start to establish yourself online.

You will naturally build your network by reaching out to new contacts and arranging shoots with different creatives (as discussed in Chapter 2.) It's not only potential clients, photographers or stylists in your network either – it's also important to reach out to hairdressers, manicurists, music PRs, set designers, art directors and advertising agencies, and anyone else in the industry you think might be useful to know in future. Just start being visible and over time you will begin to add people who follow you back on Instagram, then it's time to get those initial meetings with them in the diary.

KEEPING IN TOUCH WITH YOUR NETWORK

As you work with people, just keep in touch with them on as regular a basis as you have time for. It's up to you how you want to do this, but I use a mixture of Instagram, email and face to face or Zoom meetings to keep up with the people I know. Nothing beats meeting in real life, but meetings are very time consuming. Obviously liking someone's pictures on Instagram is not the same as meeting up, but it's still a good way to keep in touch with people and something I do whenever I have some spare time. These all have to be weighed up — how much time you will put into it based on what you will get out of it.

RECOMMENDING OTHER CREATIVES

Also, ironically in this Age of Instagram where you can find literally anyone with a scroll of your thumb, more and more people want to work with someone who has been recommended. Knowing who does good work and passing that knowledge onto people is a hugely powerful endorsement, and other creatives are very grateful when you do so. If you do recommend people that you know and like, either to join your creative teams or to do jobs that you can't, over time others will reciprocate to recommend you for other jobs. Be good to your network, and it will be good to you in return.

BUILDING RELATIONSHIPS WITH PHOTOGRAPHERS

I think that you can gather by now how important the photographers that you work with are, and that building great relationships with them will pay dividends in future. Every photographer can turn into someone you work with potentially for many years, and even become good friends.

You need to always be looking ahead to find new photographers that you would like to work with later on and use Instagram to keep track of their work and be present and active by liking their posts. Then, contact them when you feel the time is right. As I've said before, you won't always get a positive response, but you will get one sometimes and then it's up to you to see whether there is magic when you shoot together. When you are starting out, it's good to try and get in touch with assistants of established photographers you like.

BUILDING RELATIONSHIPS WITH MAKEUP BRANDS AND HOW BEAUTY PR WORKS

Luckily I feel I understand this from a fairly broad perspective since I have worked over the years of my career as a makeup artist, a beauty editor, beauty blogger, and as a social media manager for a beauty brand, as well as assisting lots of big makeup artists and as First Assistant to a celebrity makeup artist. Having said that, like every part of our industry it has also changed immeasurably with the advent of social media and will continue to do so.

At least if I can explain the basics of how beauty PR works with regards to makeup artists, it gives you an understanding of what's involved with building relationships with brands.

Makeup brands have public relations departments that work with journalists and now beauty influencers to keep their brand and products in front of consumers, to help drive sales. Obviously makeup artists can be a key market for beauty brands to target as we work with so many different products, and product recommendations from a makeup artist can be very powerful.

When I started out as a makeup artist, it was all about getting mentions for beauty brands in the print press such as magazines and newspapers, which you would get by appearing in articles about beauty products or working on editorials that you would then credit to a particular brand.

Now print media still has its place of course, but of arguably greater significance for brands is getting mentions on Instagram, TikTok and YouTube. This is where you come in. It's never been easier to build a relationship with your favourite brand by posting about them on your social media channels.

Recognition from a beauty brand obviously isn't going to happen in the next ten minutes – every brand gets thousands of mentions a day, so you need to work on it over time. But if you genuinely love a brand, and use it in your kit, and maybe show your audience how you use their products and do it consistently and in an interesting way, you will become visible to the beauty companies over time.

Especially as your social media following grows you can eventually have the potential to be given free product by the brand to test out or get invites to new launches of products. Depending on the size of your audience there can be brand collaborations further down the track as well.

Over the last few years, the relationship that brands had with makeup artists has moved considerably over to influencers and Instagrammers, and sometimes they are also makeup artists but not necessarily. They are people who love makeup, are often self-taught and have big followings on social media and YouTube. Influencers are the ones who have people's attention at the moment, which is why beauty brands have been prioritising them. This is where taking elements of successful beauty influencers to build your makeup career strategy could be useful.

MAKEUP ARTIST CREDIT PROGRAMMES

Many brands have a Makeup Credit programme in place for makeup artists, which involves makeup brands giving you products for a credit on an editorial shoot. It's a way for makeup artists to promote different brands that they use in their kit, and to get some sort of renumeration for often low-paid (or no pay) editorial. When shoots appear in magazines, the magazine will name the creative team who worked on the shoot, and allow you to mention one brand that you used the most.

We all have certain brands that are favourites in our kit, so for instance, when I do a magazine editorial, my credit reads "Makeup by Christabel Draffin using ____" and then I credit the brand that I used a lot of on that shoot. Once the magazine comes out, you can then email the brand's PR department and let them know that you've credited them in that particular editorial. They will usually send you a few products in exchange for the credit.

It does need to be certain magazine titles though, as it can't be any random magazine on the internet. The brand's PR in your country will usually prioritise titles, especially print ones, from the country that you are based in. Also getting the contact details for the brand PRs can take some time and is generally something that your network or your agent will help you with.

Building relationships with beauty PRs can take awhile, but my advice is to do the best makeup you can, then tag the brands that you used and over time the social media managers of the beauty brands will start to notice who you are.

Hint - Focus on smaller, newer brands and always do something for them first by posting about their products so they can see that you legitimately use and like their ranges. You will be a lot more visible online to a smaller brand than the giant companies like MAC or Bobbi Brown, so if you love an independent, more niche brand, say so!

CHAPTER 8

Working for Free

Starting out as a makeup artist, your first priority is to get your skills and experience up to do your job, without making any significant errors. For this you will need to work for free to build your portfolio and/or showreel, to meet people and to develop your skills to the level they need to be. You don't need to work for free forever, but you will need to do it until you feel confident you can consistently deliver on any job you get booked on.

If working without getting paid for a period of time doesn't sound like something you'd be OK with, it's not the career for you, and it's far better to know that now rather than later down the line. But there comes a point in your career when you SHOULD be getting paid when you are doing commercial work, and the trick is to know when that is, and not getting exploited.

Sometimes I think that talking about making money as a creative is like it's a dirty thing to be ashamed of – as if because makeup is your passion and you love what you do you should feel guilty to get paid for it, or to negotiate what you should be getting paid. Please disabuse yourself of this immediately if this resonates even a little bit for you. You might love doing makeup, but it is your JOB, which last time I checked involved getting paid.

No one else you know would trundle off to work as an accountant, or a waitress, or an air hostess FOR FREE every day because they say, 'I love my job!' Maybe they do love being an accountant or a waitress, but they also expect to be remunerated for their efforts. If you have any hang-ups mentally about asking for money you will need to work on it as there are plenty of people in the fashion industry who are very happy to take advantage of that as they get free labour.

If negative ideas about money mean the thought of negotiating your fee makes you feel nauseous, or you go clammy when you think of selling your skills to new people (I think we've all been there), I encourage you to start journaling and do the psychological work necessary to recognise your worth and that you deserve to get paid commensurate with the experience that you have as a makeup artist.

If this is an area you need to work on, (and I definitely did) I highly recommend Jen Sincero's book, *You Are a Badass at Making Money*. It breaks down in a very practical manner how to get over psychological blocks around money because if you have any, there is a whole raft of unscrupulous people who will be very ready to pay you less, or in fact zero, if they can get away with it.

You can see that there is a grey area with regards to the creative industries as you do need experience to improve, and in order to get this it can involve working for free for a period of time. So there's no getting around the fact that makeup artists DO need to work for free sometimes. But it's knowing when and when not to.

Please note, that the editorial that you do to build and later refresh your portfolio is also usually free, or close to it, so you're already doing a certain percentage of free work each year on your editorial to market your makeup effectively. So I'm not talking about working for free on editorial. That's a given!

When I talk about being exploited it is working for free on jobs like advertising, e-commerce or social media, company fashion shows, celebrity promotion or press junkets and jobs that are commercial. My basic rule of thumb on this is, is someone else making money from me working for free? If they are you need to think long and hard about doing it without pay.

HOW TO DECIDE WHEN IT'S WORTH WORKING FOR FREE

The best thing to do is look at what the free job you are being offered is, and whether you are already confident and experienced enough in this area that you are already charging for it or believe you should be. So, if you've already successfully done some music videos before, or directed a catwalk show, then you probably don't need to do a free day of it.

If, however it allows you to get better at your job and it's something you HAVEN'T done before, it might be worth considering. For instance, you've been offered a large TV commercial for a charity that allows you to practice what it's like heading up a big job with multiple talent to make up and assistants to manage which isn't something you have experience with, then that could be worth thinking about doing for free so you can charge for a similar job next time.

It's also important to look at the photographer who is shooting it, and who are the other members of the team (if you can find out.) From time to time it *may* be worth it to have the experience of working with a certain name photographer or stylist or to get a particular brand on your CV.

However, my experience is that once they think of you as the person who works for free, you are never going to shake that title. They are never grateful enough to change their perception of you as the 'free makeup artist' and there are often promises like "Oh next time we have more budget, we'll fly you to shoot the next campaign in the Maldives!" No. They will find more budget and pay for a more expensive team, the people who originally said no to working for free. Sad but true. ONLY do an unpaid job if there is a clear-cut benefit to you that this time around isn't money, but you think will pay dividends in your career later on. This is a business, not a hobby, and you must treat it as such. Also bear in mind that working for free has an impact on the industry as a whole – if clients think they can get great makeup for free, why would they pay next time?

HOW LONG DO I NEED TO WORK FOR FREE?

Makeup artists starting out often ask me how long they need to work for free for, and the answer is – there is no easy answer. You will always need to do free editorial, but since you love your job (because you will love your job), you won't mind since those are the days you can be as creative as you want and the results showcase your work. But for other commercial work, it depends on what type of makeup you want to do, how quickly you learn, how quickly you can get your portfolio and website done, and the experience you need, under your belt.

What I do say is you will know in your gut when you should be charging for your services. When you start to feel resentful about working for free, it's time to charge. When you sense others are profiting from your hard and excellent labour and you are simply working for free, it's time to charge.

Working for free isn't forever because eventually you will have the skills. You will go off to work one day on a job that you know you will do very well and that someone else is profiting from your unpaid labour, and you will feel sick and angry and resentful in the pit of your stomach. And you will know exactly what I mean when it happens, and on the next job like that, you will charge for it.

NON-MAKEUP JOBS YOU CAN DO WHILST YOU BUILD YOUR MAKEUP CAREER

It should be clear by now at this stage of the book that becoming a makeup artist doesn't happen overnight, and it might be necessary for you in the meantime to have a non-makeup part-time job that allows you to keep building your portfolio and skills.

Obviously working on a makeup counter is ideal as it allows you to use your makeup skills and practice whilst being at work, but this may not be an option for you, so any job that gives you some flexibility in your schedule whilst paying your bills is perfect.

If you are looking for a job that works reasonably well with makeup freelancing, perhaps think about bar or restaurant work, as it tends to be more in the evenings. This way you could potentially have makeup work in the day, and do bar or restaurant work at night.

It's also possible you could have a daytime job of any type during the week and dedicate your weekends to building your portfolio – if you are slow and methodical and consistent in your approach this is a completely viable option. The main thing to remember is that the more available for incoming makeup jobs you can be, the quicker the whole process of launching your career will be.

Or if you have other skills that would allow you to look for online work (like freelance writing, editing, graphic design or translation), you could always fit in this work around whatever makeup work you have planned. Fiverr and Upwork are two of the most famous of these websites that allow you to post all kinds of skills you might have in order to bring in freelance work you can do when you have free time. Basically, you want to try and calibrate your time so you can do as little as possible of whatever thing you do that currently makes you money, to give you maximum space in your schedule to do what you love, which if you're reading this, is your makeup.

SECTION THREE

Money

CHAPTER 9

Making Money

Deciding how you will make money in the time it takes to become a fully-fledged, self-supporting makeup artist is VERY important. Becoming a freelancer means that you no longer have a steady stream of income that you can rely on, so the planning that you do ahead of time for the inevitable ups and downs of freelance life is critical.

The old rule of thumb ten to twenty years ago is that it would take a good two – three years to get started as a fashion makeup artist in a particular market. I personally think that now due to the fact that there are many more makeup artists in the world these days, it probably takes closer to five years to get established depending on where you live in the world. By 'established' I mean that people know you, you're working about three days or more a week and you're earning some sort of living as a makeup artist. Once you reach this level you should continue to grow your earnings.

I would also like to say that if the thought of selling yourself into clients and other creatives makes you feel queasy, you are not alone. I was definitely like that for years, but it wasn't until I decided to really get my head down and start pitching myself to a lot more people that I started to earn money. Sales is a learnable skill. Believe me, I am living proof! And luckily the more that you practice it, the easier it becomes.

MAKEUP ARTIST DAY RATES

There are two types of job as a makeup artist – paid and unpaid. Paid work (also known as 'commercial' work) is generally for advertising or promotion of some kind for a brand or a celebrity, but can sometimes include editorial.

Unpaid work is usually always editorial and is needed to build your portfolio and to get to know creative teams that you can work with. As discussed in the previous chapter, working unpaid on a commercial job needs to be carefully considered as to how it will help your overall career, but is worth it for a period of time whilst you are building up your experience.

PAID WORK

I don't want to get too specific about different pay rates for different jobs as my readers live and work all over the world, thus what is a standard day rate in Capetown is not the same as in New York, or in Paris. But overall, the pay goes up in brackets and you should get paid more the more experienced you are and the higher quality your work is.

Rates can vary for shooting still photos (known as 'stills') to commercials to music videos to social media to certain editorial, or for whether you are doing makeup only, or hair and makeup on a particular job.

COMMERCIAL RATES

Generally makeup artists get paid what is known as a Day Rate. This means that they get paid for doing a day's work, which should be around 8-10 hours. You can also have jobs that are Half-Day (either in the morning or the afternoon, so around 4 hours.) However, it is common to quote a full day rate for these jobs as you will have to book yourself out for the day. Commercial jobs can vary enormously, from TV commercials with many extras, to doing a single client for a red-carpet event, and every market in the world will have different rates for each type of work. Commercial jobs will sometimes also pay overtime, which is an hourly fee paid if the shoot or job goes on longer than expected.

EDITORIAL RATES

Freelance creatives do editorial shoots – the fashion and beauty stories that you see in magazines that I described previously - to show their work. It's so that potential clients can see the type of work you do, and eventually as your work improves you will be considered for better and higher paying jobs based on this editorial. It also allows you to flex your creative muscles and to improve the standard of your makeup work.

Although a lot of editorial is unpaid, some magazines, particularly in overseas markets, will pay an editorial day rate which is usually set and non-negotiable. Italy, the UAE and China are some of the overseas markets that pay reasonably well for editorial, so it really depends where in the world you are working. Also note that magazines often commission work in other markets – thus, you could live in London and shoot with teams in London for magazines in other countries or continents, and they may pay considerably more than the editorial rates on UK magazines.

What to Charge

It can be stressful not knowing how much to charge for a certain type of job if you don't know. You don't want to overquote and lose the work, and you don't want to underquote and not get paid enough and possibly look like you have no idea what you're doing by not knowing the going rates.

The first port of call for any information is anyone in your network. If you have any other industry friends (hairdressers you work with can be handy for this), I would ask them about their rates if you feel comfortable doing so. Research what an approximate day rate for each type of job is in your area by using Google, and once you have an idea of what other people in your city are charging for that type of job, you will get better over time at working out what clients are happy to pay.

Don't forget, like anything, learning how to quote and negotiate your rates is a skill and something you will improve at over time.

This is also where social media groups or forums for creatives can come in handy. If you are already an active and trusted member (which is why it's a good idea to start building your community and online presence as soon as you can), this could be another place to ask around if you have a job you aren't sure what to charge for. By building up relationships with different members over time, you could always message them privately and ask if you aren't comfortable posting in public. This is why I advocate building your network BEFORE you need to ask them for anything – you are much more likely to get help when people already know who you are.

The parameters to know about the job before quoting your rate are:

- Timings?
- Is it shooting photography or video?
- Will you be doing makeup only, or hair and makeup?
- Is there travel required, and if so, who is paying for this?

Travel days should be paid at half-day rate where possible and all travel expenses should be covered.

Like anything, the more that you quote and negotiate your rates, the more comfortable you will become with it. The first time I had to give someone my rate I was practically hyperventilating with fear, but I can promise it gets easier the more you do it. As you become more comfortable with your skill level as a makeup artist you will also feel more confident about what to charge.

NEGOTIATE YOUR RATE
ON A COMMERCIAL JOB

The best way to start off negotiating with a client regarding rates is to ask what they normally pay. This then starts the conversation and means that you know what you're dealing with.

Rates can vary enormously depending on the size of the business you are dealing with, the health of the economy, the country or market that you're in and how established you are in the market. It's always better to give them a higher rate, which gives you room to negotiate down. This might make you feel slightly sick the first few times you do it, as asking for more money than you're used to can ring a lot of emotional money bells, but it's a necessary skill to learn. You don't want to be undercharging yourself.

You can always say that you're open to discussion on the rate which opens the door to further negotiation if you're really unsure about what to charge.

Occasionally a client will ask if they can pay you in clothes or products (this is sometimes called being paid in 'contra'.) This sometimes happens with small labels and designers, as it works out cheaper for them to pay you in this way than the money coming out of their business cashflow. If it's a designer or brand that you like it can be a great way to build your wardrobe (or your kit if it's beauty products) but bear in mind that clothes or makeup don't pay your rent each month. This needs to be weighed up against whether it's worth your while to keep loyalty with that particular team, what images you'll get out of it, the association of the brand and if you think you're just being taken advantage of!

Starting out, I'm not going to sugar coat it, most of your work will be for free whilst you build up your experience. If you've been asked to do a job that is a really low rate, you can always ask for expenses to be paid on top – this could be covering the cost of your cabs or travel to and from the shoot for instance. Be careful of doing commercial jobs for a very low rate though as it sets a precedent for later shoots with that client. It's very hard to go and charge the same client a higher rate later on as they know you agreed to do the job for a very low amount before.

HOW TO GET YOUR FIRST CLIENT

Once you feel like your book is strong enough, and you are confident with your makeup skills, it's time to start looking for clients. Then the next question becomes, how do you know when our book is strong enough? This is when yet more research comes into play. By knowing who the other makeup artists are that work in your area, and you consider to be around your level, when you feel like your work is equivalent or BETTER than someone else you consider to be a competitor and you can see they are getting paid work, you are ready to also get paid for your makeup. Instagram is a great place to keep an eye on what the equivalent artists in your area are up to.

Don't forget that already in the process of building your portfolio you've been showcasing your skills to photographers and stylists who might like to work with you again. Photographers are often the best conduit to paid work. It's always preferable for a photographer to work with a makeup artist that they know and they can recommend to a client so that's why it's so important to work with a range of different photographers.

You can also contact potential clients yourself, and for this Instagram is again the key. You can look for smaller brands on Instagram (tip – try using hashtags for businesses of particular types in the city where you work), then either direct message on Instagram or email them, introducing yourself and say that you would love to be considered to work with them in future. Then stay present on their Instagram, liking their pictures on a regular basis.

We are in an era when it has never been easier to contact small and emerging designers and businesses as now almost anyone in the world can sell online. Whether it's through Instagram, websites or Etsy, more and more small businesses are choosing to do this as an alternative to having a traditional retail shop, or are building side hustles to supplement their income. As this stock of new entrepreneurs grows, so does your pool of potential clients who might need your makeup services.

Be prepared (like everything with being a makeup artist) to message a lot of people without getting a response, it really is a numbers game. You can use hashtags to focus in on niches within certain areas – like small organic skincare brands, or silk pyjamas, or small jewellery brands. Then use Google to find whether they are in your city, and if they are, start contacting.

WORKING FOR THE MUSIC INDUSTRY

If you want to do music videos or paid work for the music industry, you could focus on finding up and coming bands and singers to contact – either get in touch with them directly on Instagram and say you'd love to do their makeup or hair and makeup (depending on your skill set) or reach out to their record label. Again, smaller independent labels will be easier to contact than the giant international ones. Also assisting makeup artists on shoots like this to get to know photographer's assistants and make contacts for shoots at your level of the industry is another option.

A note on contacting smaller companies though – the budgets might be low (and possibly non-existent) as many small companies also have small revenues. When you're starting out, this is alright as it gives you a chance to practice your negotiating skills and also allows you to build the advertising side of your portfolio and your client list. But obviously not getting paid properly forever is not the plan!

INVOICING

As with any small business, I don't need to tell you that you will need to keep good records for yourself and for the tax office in your country. You will need to provide an invoice to your clients when you do a paid makeup job. There's a lot of accounting and invoicing software now that's helpful for keeping on top of it. They aren't super expensive, and you can save on accountant fees over time. You might not even need an accountant, most of the software available is so good now.

It's also worthwhile keeping a list of all the jobs that you have done and dividing them into paid and unpaid. This way you can mark off when they have been paid. It will save you hours of trouble later on trying to figure out who has paid you and who hasn't, and also save you the embarrassment of asking clients to pay you for jobs when they already have.

CHASING LATE INVOICES

I guarantee you will need to do this at some stage and I often have assistants ask me what the right way is to do this without alienating a client, if payment is late.

I no longer have to worry about this as my amazing agent ensures prompt payment of all my invoices, but before I had an agent, I had to do late invoice chasing myself, and this is what I did:

I have a note that says '30-Day Payment Terms' on the bottom of each of my invoices. This means that the payment is due 30 days after the invoice has been issued (note that it is NOT 30 days after you have done the job. This is why invoicing as soon as you can is so important.)

Once it became overdue, I would send a pleasant email to the person I had sent the invoice too, with the original invoice attached - it's always a good idea to make things as easy as possible for people to pay you. I would ask who you could speak to in the accounts department as your invoice is now overdue.

Then I'd make a note to chase in a week if it hadn't been paid, which happened occasionally. I would keep chasing it every Monday over the next few weeks until it was paid.

It's very important to always be polite in your communications, but you can still be firm. You need to make it clear you aren't going away and you will be expecting them to honour their agreement. However, don't go in guns blazing at the beginning – you never know what's happening in someone's life. Maybe the reason they haven't paid you is that they've had a death in the family, or just had a baby or been really sick. I've only ever had one client REALLY try and get out of paying me, in twenty years. He kept saying payment would be next week, then the week after and on it went for a couple of months.

If this happens, you need to get as firm in your responses as possible without being rude, and just keep asking the same question – 'Payment still not made, when can I expect it please?' You can also cc in more people each time you send it and step up the regularity of your emails.

After a few of those emails, I started threatening legal action. This almost always does the trick. In most countries, non-payment for services rendered can be taken to the local Small Claims Court in your city – in the UK it's a fairly straightforward process and is fairly inexpensive. Usually just the threat of this happening is enough to get paid, and if not, it's over to the Small Claims Court.

Obviously legal action is a last resort, and I know it can be scary to get to that point as they won't be booking you again after you start threatening legal action. But really, who wants to have clients who don't pay you?

THE TYPES OF MAKEUP WORK YOU CAN DO TO EARN MONEY AS A MAKEUP ARTIST

- Freelance – including advertising, celebrity, red carpet, fashion shows
- Look books for designers and brands
- E-commerce
- Working on a makeup counter
- Wedding makeup artist
- Private clients
- Concierge beauty services
- Beauty Influencer/YouTuber

- Beauty Treatments - Lash extensions/Facialist/Manicurist/Spray tanning (Note that these require accredited training, particularly in the US.)

Freelance Makeup Artist

This is what I do and is my preferred type of work. This means that you have a number of photographers and clients who book you to shoot on a freelance basis, whether through an agency or independently. It can involve doing makeup for photo shoots and video shoots, advertising campaigns and commercials, editorial, celebrity, social media or online campaigns, red carpet events, fashion shows and television commercials, or a mixture of any of these.

Pros

- Always working with different people, in different places. Meeting new people all the time, no two days are ever the same. You meet all kinds of people from actors, models and musicians to sports stars, designers, influencers, activists, entrepreneurs, writers, socialites and politicians amongst others. If you like people, then being a makeup artist is an extraordinary and lovely way to meet lots of them.
- There is always something new to learn, whether it's testing out new makeup products, trying a different technique or experimenting with social media tactics or a new makeup trend, it's endlessly fascinating.
- You are your own boss. It's all on you. This is a blessing and a curse. If you can't get your Instagram above 750 followers, that's on you. If you get booked to do makeup for a magazine cover, that's on you too.
- You can turn down work you don't want to do.

- There is a very obvious progression as you go along, a virtuous circle that builds on itself. As you work with better and better photographers you get increasing opportunities and start getting chosen for higher paid commercial jobs, which is a great feeling.

Cons

- Inconsistent income. You never know from one month to the next how much you will earn. No sick pay or holiday leave, so you have to make sure you always have savings to get you through those things as well as any tough economic times which do inevitably happen occasionally.
- Can be very tiring, as you work in different areas/studios every day and it can involve travel or location work. Particularly if you have fluctuating energy due to health problems (like I used to), it can sometimes be a tough pace to handle when you're really busy.
- No job stability. It's always shifting and changing – the market changes, your jobs are never the same, you are constantly dealing with admin and unpredictable schedules and your network is always moving and expanding.
- Admin. Lots and lots of admin. Even having an agent doesn't excuse you from the constant onslaught of PR emails, social media, updating your website and portfolio, meeting requests and keeping up with your network.
- Work can be very last minute. And in fact, the best jobs that take you to the next level are often super last minute because someone else was unavailable. So, you always need to be packed and ready to work at a moment's notice.

How do I get Freelance Makeup Work?

Either through an agent if you have one, or through your own marketing and networking efforts in your local fashion industry. (This is partly due to your portfolio building work, and also networking.)

Look Books for Designers or Brands

Traditionally twice a year, or more for the bigger brands, designers want to shoot their new collections for their websites and now to create regular Instagram content. The day rate for this has dropped in the last few years, but they are still good regular clients to have. It's usually hair and makeup for these jobs.

Pros

- Can be regular work if they continue to re-book you.
- Can be a nice way to work with new photographers if the brand works with different photographers each season or build on relationships with a team you already work well with.

Cons

- These shoots tend to happen a couple of times a year so are not that often.
- Budgets are generally not that high for look books.

How Do I Get Look Book Work?

You can either contact brands directly through Instagram - this can work well for smaller brands that have the decision maker/owner running their Instagram accounts. Larger brands will have totally separate people running their Instagram accounts (so there is no point Instagram direct messaging a big company like Zara or TopShop about shooting for them.) Also, photographers and stylists in your network will often eventually put you forward for this work with their clients if they like working with you.

E-commerce

E-commerce makeup work is working on shoots that appear on websites to show the clothes and products that are available on the brand's website. As you can imagine, the volume of pictures that need to be shot each day is very large, and as almost all brands have websites to sell online now there is more and more of this work available in most capital cities. Many people in fashion earn at least part of their living from shooting e-commerce occasionally, or sometimes full-time.

The days are usually 9am-5pm, plus you get a lunchbreak of an hour. The makeup work itself is generally not too complicated, and often it's hair and makeup, as it's cheaper for the company to have one person to do both. You do need to have both pretty strong hair and makeup skills for e-commerce.

Pros

- It can be regular work, and thus regular income.
- Tends to be the same type of hair and makeup – usually fairly natural for most high street brands and department stores. Always thoroughly check what a brand's æsthetic looks like before working with them for the first time though. And if you aren't sure about a brief, take your full kit. There are no prizes for leaving something at home that you later need on a job!
- The hours are usually 9-5, no shooting until 3am because the photographer loves working around the clock.

Cons

- It can be tiring as you shoot a lot of images in a day, and you have to reach your image quota for the day.
- Generally, not very creative. Brands don't usually want any experimental makeup looks for e-commerce, although obviously it depends on the brand.
- Usually, brands will put a number of makeup artists on hold for each shoot day, and then release the people they don't want once they have someone booked. They often

only release you the day before so it can be difficult to book other things in around e-commerce holds. (A 'hold' is a provisional booking for that particular day so that you don't then commit to working for someone else. Once it has been decided by the client that you are the makeup artist that they want on the day, the hold is confirmed and it means it's locked in.)
- Usually both hair and makeup is required.
- Very competitive and finding the people who are booking e-commerce jobs can be difficult.
- If you get a regular brand to work with, or a number of e-commerce brands you work with, it can be hard to transition out of that regular lower paying work into less consistent but higher paying work because you don't have the time available to make other connections/have meetings/shoot editorial.
- It doesn't pay as much as doing other types of freelance makeup work - advertising or red carpet for instance.

How Do I Get E-commerce Work?

Full-time makeup roles at a brand (like ASOS) will be advertised on job sites like indeed.co.uk, or also on linkedin.com. If you are looking for occasional e-commerce work you will need to look for high street brands that sell their products online using pictures where the models' faces are visible (it's important to check this as some brands crop the pictures on their website to the chin, so don't need makeup artists or hairdressers to work for them.)

The very best way to get e-commerce work is to ask around your network as you start to build your network up. One of the hairdressers or photographers you work with may be happy to recommend you if they are working at a brand doing e-commerce.

You can also look for contact details for either a producer or a production co-ordinator at that brand by using Google or LinkedIn and email them with your portfolio details and asking if you could be considered for future work. Be warned – those contact email details can be hard to find. But if you put some time into it you should get a few options to contact.

Working on a Makeup Counter

Many makeup brands sell either through counters in department or stand-alone stores and need a staff of makeup artists to apply and sell products to customers. It can be a great way to get paid to do makeup and build up your experience.

Pros

- Working for one brand, so you usually work at the same counter or stores and have regular workmates.
- Depending on the brand you can have opportunities to do the shows and assist some of the world's best makeup artists at the various fashion weeks around the world. NARS, MAC and Charlotte Tilbury, amongst other brands, all sponsor different designer's shows. They will put a team together from the brand who will then get to work under the Makeup Director who is an amazing global artist like Tom Pecheux or Diane Kendal.
- It provides a steady paycheck.
- Some brands are flexible with work hours so you may be able to do some freelance work also. You should check this before you start though as every company is different and some brands won't let you swap shifts or move the days around that you are booked to work on counter, which can make freelancing difficult.
- Paid sick days, holidays and other company benefits are available, which is not something that you have as a freelancer.
- There will be a staff discount to buy makeup which will help you build your kit.

- Counter work is amazing for experience in terms of getting all types of skin, ethnicities and personalities in your chair.
- Can be a great way to meet brides and people who could become regular clients.
- You can also progress through the company into training roles and many have National or International Artist roles that means that you can travel the country or internationally working on shoots and shows.

Cons

- You need to be great at selling product. Obviously, you need to be proficient at applying makeup, but if you can't sell the products to customers you won't get hired.
- Sales quotas can be aggressive depending on the company so it can be stressful to hit them every day.
- May not be able to move your shifts so it can be hard to work on your portfolio - some brands are more flexible than others and may let you swap your shifts with other people.
- Pay is slightly more than minimum wage. You will need to work quite a lot of hours to earn enough to live in most places.

How Do I Get Work on a Makeup Counter?

By using job ads on jobseeker websites, or LinkedIn.com to find out who is hiring, you can then contact the companies with your details.

If you don't have previous makeup sales experience it can be hard to get a first makeup counter job, but a good tip is to use YouTube as people post videos of how to do well in the job interviews for different brands (usually the job interviews will require you to do a trial makeup to show your work as well as to test your sales ability on selling product.) Another option is to apply to work at a brand before the Christmas period when they take on a lot more casual staff.

Wedding Makeup Artist

Applying makeup for members of a bridal party for a wedding, which usually includes the bride as well as bridesmaids and mother of the bride.

Pros

- It's mainly weekend work.
- It's usually two days' work as you get paid for the wedding trial (where you test out what products you will use on the bride on the actual wedding day) as well, which is mostly done a number of weeks/months before the wedding.
- The timeframe on a wedding can be 6-12 months so you're locking in work far in advance. It can be very helpful to know what your cashflow will look like months ahead of time.
- Wedding makeup work can be a good option for makeup artists with children as their partner, family or a babysitter can look after the kids whilst they work doing weddings on the weekends.
- It's usually seasonal, as there tend to be more weddings in the spring and summer months.
- If you live in a part of the world where people travel for weddings, you can be a destination wedding makeup artist, for instance in the South of France or Mexico. Some clients will also fly you to where the wedding is, depending on their budget.
- Great experience doing people of all ages, races and skin types although obviously you need to be pretty proficient and confident at makeup before you start looking for paid wedding work, since it is one of the biggest day's in a bride's life. The stakes are high.

Cons

- Weekend work and often in summertime.
- Brides can be lovely but can also be stressful. They will usually be very nervous and there can be family tensions and dynamics that come out on the day that you will have to smoothly negotiate.
- You need to be calm, unflappable, and good at handling stressed people.
- Time management and being fast is important as you might have quite a few members of the bridal party to do plus the bride, and no bride wants to be late for her wedding because the makeup artist took forever.
- It's a very competitive field but can be lucrative.

How Do I Get Wedding Makeup Work?

As I mentioned previously, Facebook can be a great way to get brides and I advise you to look into Facebook and Instagram ads if you want to spend some money marketing your bridal business. (You can learn all about this from YouTube videos as Facebook and Instagram advertising can seem a bit complicated at first but work really well once you get it right. There are a number of bridal marketing experts now on YouTube who have a wealth of information on advertising to brides.)

Having a separate Instagram for your bridal work is another great way to build a client base for your bridal makeup too. Word of mouth will be very powerful as you do more weddings, as bridal makeup is one of the things people like to get personal recommendations on. Another good tip is to partner with a wedding planner, wedding photographer, florist, wedding dress boutique or bridal hairdresser in your area and you can refer each other clients. You could also look at doing makeup tutorials on Instagram TV/Reels to promote your bridal work. Finally make sure you have nice business cards printed and keep them on you at all times so you can give them to prospective brides when asked.

Private Clients

This is when people need makeup for special events, so it could be for parties, dinners, lunches, work functions, red carpets, christenings, graduation or Prom, bar and bat mitzvahs, Christmas or New Year's Eve parties, or Halloween. It can be a great way to make money if you can get regular work in this field.

For the lower end of the market you are usually competing with the makeup counters, where people get their makeup done and the fee payable is redeemable in product, thus it's pretty difficult to compete with that in terms of price. It's usually better to focus on the more premium end of the market in wealthy areas, especially private clients who go out regularly to different events.

Pros

- Generally, it only takes a couple of hours maximum to do the makeup.
- Usually weekend or evening work so it can work well with children or if you have another half day job on in the mornings.
- You can choose which clients you work with.
- It's often repeat business.
- Doing one person in a social circle often leads to other referrals to their friends.

Cons

- Even if it is only a couple of hours you still need to block out the travel time for it, so it usually ends up being a half day even if it's only one person.
- Getting new clients can be difficult.
- It's usually not very consistent work as most people might only want you once or twice a year.
- Certain days of the week or times of the year you will be over-booked - NYE, Saturday nights, Halloween for instance - and other times of the year can be very quiet.

How Do I Get Private Clients?

Getting more private clients is similar to brides in that it's about getting booked by women who need makeup done for an event. Partnering with a local hair or beauty salon to grow your client base can be useful, as well as using Facebook and Instagram pages dedicated to your private client services to find people and market your work (See my information above on getting more bridal clients.)

Paying for Facebook/Instagram advertising can also be a good way to build your client base for private clients. As with all your marketing, make sure you track your results and see what is working for you and what isn't. Using local hashtags can be good as well – say you live in Surrey in the UK, try using the hashtag #surreymakeupartist to promote your services. Finally you could also look at doing makeup tutorials on Instagram TV or Reels to show your work and increase your audience. Make sure you have nice business cards printed and keep them on you at all times so you can give them to prospective clients when asked.

Concierge Beauty Services

There are beauty concierge services in many capital cities now, where people can book a makeup artist/hairdresser and/or manicurist to come to their homes to do their makeup for events. Blow in London is an example of this type of service.

Pros

- Will give you great experience of all different skin tones, types and client preferences.
- Will make you very fast as you don't have long generally to get the client ready.
- Will provide you with a steady stream of clients – you don't need to have your own marketing set up, it's all done through their app and the company does all the marketing for you.
- You can work the days that suit you just by using their app to say you're available and they will start sending you clients once you have been set up in their system.

Cons

- They generally don't pay extremely well.
- You use your own products which can get expensive.
- Many of these services are both hair and makeup as well, so you will be expected to have strong skills in each.
- You need to be relatively experienced already before you start working for these services.
- Getting to clients in a capital city with your kit can be tiring, and stressful as well depending on transport links and traffic.

How Do I Get Concierge Makeup Work?

Google 'concierge beauty services' or 'beauty on demand' + the city in which you live to find a range of business that offer concierge beauty services, then contact them with your portfolio and CV. You can also check their company page on LinkedIn.com for whether they are hiring.

Beauty Influencer/YouTuber

The success of influencers and YouTubers has been a huge change in the beauty landscape in the last decade. The explosion of social media and online platforms where makeup artists can literally build their own audience has transformed how makeup artists can market themselves and their work. The tools to create this kind of success are not only widely available but extremely low cost, so this can be a very viable route to market. The online influencers are now the ones with the brand contracts and relationships with brands and PRs - and making a fortune in the process.

But let me be clear: being a beauty influencer is a full-time job, so it will require a lot of effort to build up that part of your career and may be difficult to juggle with freelance fashion shoots, but not impossible.

Obviously if you do well on YouTube there are great rewards, but it also can be very stressful as you need to be constantly generating quality content for your fans, and the percentage of successful YouTubers to unsuccessful is vanishingly small. In fact, Fortune.com published an article in 2018 that stated that 96.5% of people starting out as YouTubers won't make enough money from advertising in a year to crack the US poverty line. This doesn't mean that you won't be part of the 3.5% who do well on YouTube, but it's worth being aware of that statistic going into it as it can look like it would be easy and fun and a quick way to riches, which is not the case as it's so incredibly competitive.

Note: Shooting beauty videos for Instagram TV/Reels is becoming rapidly more popular now as it's less technically difficult than YouTube and leverages whatever audience you already have. TikTok is also another platform which can also potentially be hugely successful for makeup artists, so might be worth thinking about testing out.

Pros

- Global recognition if you succeed.
- A way of showing what you do to prospective clients and brands. Having your own audience is always helpful to being a successful makeup artist.
- Brands increasingly seem more inclined to give global beauty contracts to makeup artists with their own online following - Lisa Eldridge and French makeup artist Violette both garnered global cosmetic contracts after starting their YouTube channels.
- Money. There is big money to be made if you build a popular channel. However, don't expect to be successful unless you put in a LOT of unpaid work. Uploading a video once a month won't cut it. Generally speaking the more content you can put out the better.
- After you have built a following, brands will send you product to review for free and it could help you build your kit.

- In time it can be a great platform to sell your own products, whether it's makeup or skincare or in the case of Lisa Eldridge, her own lines of jewellery and lipsticks. There is also the possibility of brand collaborations where an existing brand will contact you to put your name on some of their products, such as @nikki_makeup and her collaboration with Sweed eyelashes.

Cons

- You will usually need to do it for free for a really long time whilst you build your audience. In time you will build an audience, but it can take ages - think years rather than months unless you hit on something that is an instant hit and immediately goes viral. Most successful YouTubers say they posted videos for at least two years to a handful of people before their numbers started to take off.
- Certain types of makeup and YouTubers do better than others. You won't know if you are one of them until you try. Being attractive and/or funny or having a specific niche that you can do better than anyone else obviously helps you to build your audience faster.
- The amount of work involved with being a YouTuber does make it hard to also be a full-time fashion makeup artist. There are a few famous makeup artists who do it, (such as Violette, Hung Vanngo and Monika Blunder) but they aren't creating all that content on their own. They aren't dealing with technical problems and also being on-set on Italian Vogue; they have a team to help them deliver content and allow them to balance having a YouTube career with editorial makeup. However, it's not impossible to do it so go for it if you think it's of interest.
- Mental health can become an issue – many influencers are now suffering burnout due to the relentless pressure of always, always needing to be generating constant content. As soon as you stop posting, your stats start dropping so mentally it can be difficult to deal with that continuous

pressure of always needing to be broadcasting something. Google the YouTuber Michelle Phan if you want a cautionary tale – she was the world's top YouTuber/beauty influencer in 2010 and disappeared from the online world in 2016 for a period of time after suffering from intense depression and burnout.

○ Managing the PR relationships and brands plus the amount of product you receive is surprisingly time consuming. I know this sounds like a problem many people would love to have, but when I had a beauty blog a few years ago it started to take up a huge amount of my time either writing posts, meeting with brands, testing the products, dealing with the mountains of emails and networking with other bloggers. A word of advice – if you don't love it, you won't be able to keep up with the amount of work involved.

It is possible to take elements of what successful influencers do and use those to grow your social media, without becoming a full-time influencer – some fashion makeup artists do tutorials and makeup breakdowns on their Instagram which can work really well for them. Have a look at what other makeup artists are doing, and then test out different elements of their strategy to see if it works for you.

How Do I Become a Beauty Blogger/Influencer?

You will need to start creating very regular content and posting it to your channel(s). The good news is that it can be cheap to get started - just an internet connection, a ring light and an iPhone is enough to get going, although you may want to upgrade to better photographic equipment later on. As I said before, start with you what you have and take it from there.

Beauty Therapist – Facialist/Lash Extensions/Brow Expert/Spray Tanning/Manicurist

Any other beauty treatments that you offer will usually require specialist training and licensing, so it is essential you check the accreditations required where you live. I would also recommend that you market them separately to your other makeup work, but they can be a nice addition to what you offer as a makeup artist, and an extra income source.

Pros

- Flexibility, as most treatments you can get the client to come to you, or you could offer mobile services and go to them.
- You can choose the hours that you work if you work for yourself (and not in a salon) so if you have kids it can fit in well with looking after them, particularly if they are school age.
- Being a manicurist is a particularly useful skill set to have as it fits in well with your editorial makeup work.

Cons

- It requires special training and in most parts of the world accreditation in order to provide those services to the public.
- It's another business, with a different clientele and you will need to market that as well as your fashion makeup business.

How Do I Get Beauty Treatment Work?

First you need to do whatever training is required where you live to safely and legally provide the service you wish to advertise. Then like getting private clients and brides, I would recommend a combination of Facebook and Instagram advertising as well as building up your social media audience in the geographical area you want to work in by using local hashtags (such as #londonfacial, #spraytanlondon.)

CHAPTER 10

Managing Your Expenses

CONTROLLING YOUR EXPENSES

Ah yes, the unsexy 'budgeting' word. You knew it was coming, didn't you? One of the best things you can do as a freelancer (not just as a makeup artist) is getting on top of your expenses. Of course, that's not to say you can't be successful if you don't know what money you have coming in and out, but I personally found it amazingly helpful to really look at my expenses and understand my financial priorities and how much work I needed to do to in order to cover my monthly bills.

If you know exactly how much money you need to have coming in, you can work out how many days you need to have paid jobs per week or month in order to cover your expenses. This then can become your monthly target to work towards for paid/commercial makeup work.

Without having a proper budget, I think it's very difficult to have concrete ideas of where you want your makeup to be in one year or five years. Having a set amount of money you know you need to bring in each month really focuses the mind and helps to make decisions about what you do (and don't!) want to do.

Budgeting

YOUR BASIC BUDGET

Having a proper budget for what you will need to earn to cover your basic living expenses will allow you to see whether the income you have coming in from your makeup is sufficient to cover these needs.

It's best to initially create a 'bare bones budget' which covers the absolute essentials that you need to pay for to keep your personal show on the road – things like rent, food, internet and mobile phone and basic transport expenses should all be covered so you know the minimum amount you need to get by.

Then when you know what type of work you're doing, and how much a standard day typically pays, you know how many days' paid work you need to bring in to support yourself. Then all the other things you have to do (like portfolio building/editorial) can slot around your paid work. This gives you concrete goals to work towards as you build your makeup career that are based around supporting yourself financially as soon as possible on the journey.

BUDGETING SOFTWARE

I know budgeting is one of the most fearsome words in the English language – everybody hates the thought of it. But take it from someone who was an indiscriminate, profligate spender for most of her life (think Carrie Bradshaw but less sensible), getting to grips with the money you have flowing in and out of your life will make you a lot more relaxed and able to spend on the things that matter to you most.

About four years ago, I discovered a life changing budgeting software and at the risk of sounding like a giant nerd, I actually love my budget now. The software program is called You Need a Budget, or YNAB for short, and it literally changed my life. And no, this isn't #sponsored or an #ad, I've just used and loved it since I found it. It can be found at Ynab.com, and it's not hard to use, plus they have lots of online support and how-to videos to get you started.

The beauty of the YNAB software is it's very flexible for freelancers as it only asks you to budget the money you have right now. Not the money you hope you might have, or that Grandma Marjie could be sending in your Christmas card like she does every year, but the actual money you have in your account right now. Which you then can allocate to different categories - which might include coffee, and wine and yes, makeup, but maybe sponsoring that alpaca in Peru may need to wait this month. Or maybe the wine can wait, and the alpaca gets the cash, but being able to see what money you have available is a game changer.

YNAB allows you to move money around if you overspend in a category, meaning you don't need to feel like a failure when the inevitable happens and you run out of money in a category. You just have to pull it from another category. So, you realise that money isn't infinite, and whether you have a lot coming in or a little, you need to make choices with the money you have on hand. It also helps you to get out of debt if that's where you're at right now (no shame on that topic either, I think we've all been there too.)

It also allows you to save regularly for those irregular bills that do come in, like taxes, or an unexpected car repair or vet bill. That way the money is set aside, in a small amount each month, and when something unexpected happens you've already got the funds allocated for it meaning you don't need to panic or go into debt to pay for surprise expenses.

HAVING AN EMERGENCY FUND

So, the beauty of having a budget and controlling your expenses means you can build up an Emergency Fund. This is one of the most essential things in any makeup artist's kit, quite frankly. Better than any concealer! It gives you peace of mind and is a way of preparing for life's unexpected difficulties which happen to us all occasionally.

This Emergency Fund will save you from going into debt when things go wrong, or work is not that plentiful.

How much is the right amount to save? This differs for everyone, but I think at least a couple of months' worth of all your expenses should be saved on a cash account that you can easily access if something unexpected happens. Some people like to have up to three months' worth of expenses put away, for others it's closer to twelve months, but you'll have to decide what feels like the right amount for you.

As you can imagine, it will take you some time to save this up, and that's fine. By consistent budgeting, you will be able to get on top of your monthly expenses which is a great skill to have later on to get you through the lean times that do come occasionally.

The idea is that you spend less than you earn, (not rocket science I know, but still it can be surprisingly hard to do), and then put the extra money away into your Emergency Fund. Then once this Emergency Fund is at the level that you'd like, you can start saving for other things like fun stuff such as holidays, or longer-term priorities like houses and retirement.

The best way to do this is to set up a regular weekly or monthly payment from your everyday bank account into a special dedicated savings account so it just gets deducted automatically every week or month. Then allow it to build and never turn off that automatic contribution. That way, even if you need to dive into your Emergency Fund to cover something unexpected, it just fills back up again after the emergency is over, ready for the next time you need it.

I lost one of my biggest clients a couple of years ago since they went in-house for their creative work and stopped using the agency that I used to work with, which meant that a good percentage of my monthly income disappeared overnight, through no fault of my own. That focused my mind wonderfully and I put feelers out to my network, looking for any and every opportunity I could. I even started to look at café jobs, or work on a makeup counter, but luckily I got a big two-day ad job that literally saved my bacon. (And meant I didn't have to actually sling bacon.)

Which just goes to show, you never know when the tide will turn, and the next big job will come in. This is why I am such a fan of looking ahead and pre-empting problems before they arrive, to give you the time you need for the good stuff to happen – because sometimes success is just around the corner.

CREATING A KIT BUDGET

Ah, another big question – how do I budget to build a kit? Just so you know, building your kit never really goes away, even after you have a good basic kit organised. There are always things that need replacing or updating in any artist's kit. And building a makeup kit is EXPENSIVE. Even after applying for artist discounts - many brands do have pro artist schemes in place which are definitely worth signing up for - there is still a lot to buy before you can even start working.

In addition to makeup, brushes, wipes, tissues and perhaps hair products for your hair kit, there are also sturdy bags needed to transport your kit, set bags as well as false eyelashes, skincare and nail products – the list goes on. A kit is always a work in progress so you don't need to panic about getting everything at once, but a plan to buy what you need over time is a good idea as it can feel a bit overwhelming to start with.

I'm not going into the details of what you should buy here as its out of the scope of this book, but even after your kit is pretty organised, there are always things that need replenishing. Body moisturiser, body makeup, razors for male grooming, mascara – there is always something that is running out that needs replacing. That's before you even get into the fun stuff, like new lip or eyeshadow colours. Your kit is never really 'done'. I still have a kit budget, and I've been doing makeup for twenty years.

The best way I have found to deal with this and not go overboard with buying makeup (which can be tempting, especially when you're starting out), is to set a monthly makeup budget. Thus, you have an amount you allow yourself each month to buy things for your kit. Obviously when you're starting out this will probably be fairly small, whatever you can afford. Then over time and you earn more money, you can allocate a greater amount of money if you wish. This pushes you to make decisions about what you need most and not go crazy buying ALL THE THINGS, many of which you may not end up using. (Speaking from experience here, people.)

Once you have a decent set of brushes, foundations and powders for ALL skin tones and skincare organised, I would start adding basic colours – neutral eyeshadows and lipsticks and blushes, basic eyeliners. Then as you and your work progress you can start adding a wider variety of colours and products based on the type of work and jobs that you find you are doing.

Take it from someone who bought a lot of makeup when she was starting out 'just in case', you need to find your way a bit in your career before you go mad at the makeup counter. Buy feathered eyelashes and neon paints and glitter gel eyeliner as you need them, almost on a job by job basis. That way you are building your kit over time and figuring out what you like and need, and what you don't.

BUYING FOUNDATIONS

Foundations are one of the most expensive things you purchase when you are building your kit, so I discovered a good hack recently to help you choose which foundation ranges to test out when you are looking at which ones to buy for your kit.

Now pretty much all the makeup brands do testers for their ranges of bases in little pots so that you can check out what they are like at home, rather than buying five bottles of something and then finding out you don't like it. Just tell the salesperson that you're a makeup artist and thinking about buying it for your kit but you would like a couple of testers to try first for different skin tones. I would recommend asking for one in your skin tone so you can test it on yourself, and another couple in different shades that you can test on friends or family.

It's brilliant to be able to try foundations before you buy as some products can perform very differently on different types of skin. This is something you want to know BEFORE you invest hundreds of pounds/dollars in a range of foundation you don't end up using because you don't like it, or it has inconsistent performance.

CHEAPER MAKEUP RANGES

The good news when building your kit is that there are many excellent cheaper makeup brands around now and you can also get decent starter products from brands at the cheaper end of the market like NYX, Sleek or Kiko for example. Which means that you can build a good basic kit for a lot less money than it took when I started out and there were only premium brands like MAC, Shu Uemura, Chanel, Bobbi Brown and the more expensive brands to choose from.

Also, you can now do so much research online with YouTube and beauty bloggers – for any product you are thinking of buying there are multiple reviews and whole videos dedicated to whether they are good or not. Some in-depth research up-front means you can work out what brands really do perform consistently and what's worth spending money on, before you actually spend the money on them.

A FINAL RECOMMENDATION

If you currently have consumer debt (credit cards or personal loans apart from a mortgage), I strongly advocate paying this off as quickly as you can. As you have gathered so far from this book, being a freelancer is about being flexible and having debt reduces your financial flexibility in that you always need to earn a certain amount each month, just to make the minimum payments on that debt. That's before you even start on having enough for your monthly expenses.

Debt makes you vulnerable when the inevitable things in life happen, such as time off needed to look after a sick child, a car repair or you are injured and can't work. If you are already paying off debt it makes it likely you will end up even deeper in more debt to pay for the latest problem. The less stress you have financially the easier the freelance life is.

CHAPTER 11

Taxes and Insurance

PAYING TAXES

Again, as this book is not specific to any one country, I can't get into too much detail about the tax laws of each place. But what is for sure is that you will be required to pay taxes on your makeup artist earnings at some point in your career. As a freelancer taxes don't automatically get deducted from your pay as they do when you work for a company, so you need to arrange to have the money set aside for these ahead of time, before the Tax Office comes calling.

PUTTING MONEY ASIDE TO PAY TAX

A word to the wise – don't spend all the money you earn and then have to dread tax time as you don't have your tax money already set aside. Especially if you've had a good year of earnings your tax bill can run into tens of thousands of dollars/pounds if you're a really successful makeup artist, and I've heard more than one horror story of artists needing to scramble to get that money in a few weeks to pay the tax department as they didn't have it already put away.

Don't let this be you! The best way is to have a separate account for your tax, and EVERY time you get paid for a makeup job, put the required percentage of money away, for whatever tax bracket you are in. You can find out from Google how much you should be paying each year depending on what country you're in, and what tax bracket you are in. That way that money is set aside ready for tax day, because friends, it's coming for all of us, every year, without exceptions.

TRACK YOUR EXPENSES FOR YOUR TAXES

Keep track of all your receipts for the makeup that you buy and check the available deductions in your country for taxis/travel/magazines/ makeup/ tissues/ wipes/Q-tips and so forth, that you spend each year to keep yourself in business.

Either get a tax accountant who specialises in the fashion industry to help you with your tax return, or Google what deductions are available in your country for makeup artists. You might be surprised at what you can deduct. As always, keep it legal as ripping off the Tax Department is never a good idea, and seek professional advice from a registered tax accountant in your country if you aren't sure about something.

INSURANCE FOR MAKEUP ARTISTS

There are three types of insurance for makeup artists, and yes, they are a good idea to have. They aren't very expensive – between £50 and £100 a year if you live in the UK and for the peace of mind they offer they are definitely worth it.

Public Liability/Indemnity Insurance

This is insurance that covers you if something goes wrong when you're doing makeup (for instance, a model or client has an allergic reaction to what you used or develops a cold sore after you do their makeup.) It also covers you for damages, say someone trips on your kit suitcase and breaks their leg, or you burn a valuable antique in a location house with a hot curling iron. As you can imagine, sometimes things do go wrong at work, which is when you want to have insurance to cover yourself.

Makeup Kit Insurance

It's also possible to get insurance to cover the cost of your kit getting lost or stolen, which in addition to public liability insurance is a very sensible investment. I know makeup artists who have had their whole kits go permanently missing whilst travelling, or one makeup artist I know who had her kit stolen from her car. If the cost of replacing everything in your kit would create major financial difficulties for you or be the end of your career, it's definitely worth having Kit and Equipment Protection insurance. Note that if you take this insurance that itemizing and photographing all the products and brushes in your kit is a very good investment of time, as it will make life much easier if you have to make a claim at some point. Keeping the receipts for each item of makeup you have bought for your kit is also worthwhile.

Income Protection Insurance

This is insurance that covers you for periods of time when you can't work, perhaps due to illness or an accident. As I mentioned earlier, if there is anything wrong with your health or you break an arm or leg and are unable to work, there is no money coming in, so having a policy that covers you for loss of income in those times can give valuable peace of mind. Income Protection insurance has been a financial life saver for more than one of my freelance friends.

SECTION FOUR

Looking Ahead

CHAPTER 12

Time Management and Organisation

This is another incredibly important part of being a makeup artist and I think can be challenging for many people as our days are completely unstructured, unless you're working on a makeup job that day. Which means that you have to really have a level of self-discipline to stop yourself procrastinating and avoiding the necessary work needed to push your career along.

So how to manage your time off when you're not shooting? Because until you're fully established, and at the monthly income level that you're happy with, your free time is not really free time as there is always something you could be doing to promote yourself, and get more work coming in.

It took me many years to figure this out as the trick is to do enough to get or keep everything rolling, but not enough to end up getting ill or run down from overwork. Because as a creative freelancer, you COULD literally be working 24/7. You probably have way too many good ideas for the amount of time you have to execute them, and this is doubly true if you have children to juggle as well or are also working another job as well as building your makeup business.

Since I'm a bit of a workaholic, in previous years I found I was grinding myself into the ground with totally unrealistic expectations about what I could achieve in a day. Multiple meetings? Check. Yes, to all the jobs? Check. Hours of Instagram a day? Check and double check. I was trying to do way too many things and became quite burnt-out in the process.

So, I did what any sensible exhausted and crispy brain fried person would do and took myself off on holidays, and whilst lounging by the pool in the sun, I did some analysis. I promptly discovered many of the extra hours I put in weren't as productive as I would like. I felt like all my time I was always either working, prepping for work, thinking about work or doing social media and emails. That, my friends, is no way to live.

Every one of you is in a totally different place in your career so I can't give you a one size fits all approach to time management, but I can give you some principles that have helped me over the years to design the most productive schedule for me.

- Once time is gone, you can't get it back. This is terrifying but also liberating. You can't buy or make more of it, so spend it wisely.
- Be clear about what your next goals are. Do you want to get your initial portfolio done? Reach a certain number of Instagram followers? Get editorial in certain magazine titles? Reach a particular amount of income every month? Build a bridal business as well as your fashion career? Increase your paid workdays each month? Having an idea of what your next concrete goal is will help you to keep taking the necessary steps to get there.
- Prioritising one or at most two things is the surest way to make sure that they happen. If you try and do all the things you will end up exhausted and often chasing your tail, getting caught up in busy work. Figure out what you're trying to achieve and a rough plan to get there, then figure

out how much free time you have to put into it and WORK THE PLAN. Once you hit that first goal, move onto the next.

- You will need to adjust as you go along, because I can tell you right now that certain goals which seem straightforward can take a lot longer to achieve than expected, as they generally involve other people. Things like getting magazine commissions, securing new photographers to work with, and meeting with creative agencies are difficult to quantify in terms of how long it will take you to get done. It may be quick, it might take months of consistent effort depending on the particular goal and how many other people are involved in achieving it, but your job is to keep at it. Keep building your portfolio and your skills and your body of work until you start to achieve the bigger goals you set yourself. As you move through your career, the next step will start to unfold and become obvious. You don't need to see the whole path laid out in front of you to get started.
- Track your time periodically for a week to see how you are spending your time, and what percentage of that time is working on the right things that are moving you closer to your goals. Every time I do this I'm always shocked by how much time slips away on things that I don't think are that important (emails, administration tasks, household maintenance, getting changed into my workout gear, that always seems to take forever and I have no idea why??) even though I do try to be pretty strict with myself with my time keeping.
- Use a timer on your phone to keep you on task if you have to do something fairly un-fun but necessary like send new business emails, or work on your website.
- It's really helpful to figure out how long certain tasks take. I now know how long a particular number of emails will take to send, or how long a mood board will take me to put together, or how long meetings or packing my kit generally takes. That way over a week I can make sure I have enough

time to do all the things that are important and drive me to my longer-term goals.
- Lists. I'm a huge fan of lists to keep track of everything in my life as there can be a lot of moving components in having multiple shoot projects constantly on the go as well as marketing and life admin.

ANALYSING WHAT'S WORKING

Something I know for sure about being a makeup artist is that the feedback from what you do can take a long time between putting the work in and getting the result back.

Often, it's only by looking back months or even YEARS later that I could I tell what had worked and what hadn't. What photographers have given me work? And consistently? What shoots in my portfolio did I get the best feedback on from clients? What magazine titles helped me get more work? Sometimes it's jobs that at the time may not have felt that important that end up being the gamechangers in your career.

Try and check your progress regularly to get a feel for what you think is working, and what maybe isn't. I find a quarterly review is always helpful. Often the results can be different to what you expected they would be. You do a major magazine and think that it's the next level of your career, and it isn't. You do a job that you nearly said no to, and it turns into one of the most important working relationships of your life.

By being intentional about next steps and having concrete actions you are taking you can see immediately if your approach is working, and you are doing the necessary work or not. Then you can adjust if you aren't getting the results you would like. If you aren't, you can give yourself a stern talking to as to why.

The more deliberate and planned you are with what you are trying to achieve, the more you can pace yourself and have the time to do the important things not just for you career, but making sure you have time to exercise, and yes, enjoy the ride along the way.

ALWAYS SAY YES

Which leads me to an important note – when starting out, whenever possible, always say yes. 'No' should not be in your vocabulary whilst you build your experience. You never know where a shoot will go, or where the people you are working with could end up.

This year's assistant photographer could be shooting the cover of i-D the following year (and actually we're in a time where superstar young photographers can emerge from what feels like nowhere.) Just say yes and do the work. You will know in your gut when you should start saying no and being more selective because that time does come in all careers, where what you turn down becomes as important as what you say yes to. However, starting out, the only word you need in your vocabulary is YES.

BEING ORGANISED

Something that isn't discussed that often about being a makeup artist is how important it is to have systems to keep track of your work and all the specifics that go along with being a makeup artist.

Being a makeup artist is a very details oriented job – managing an ever-shifting schedule, a kit, all the contacts in your network as well as finding time for a personal life whilst you are fully occupied on set for many hours each week is not easy.

I wasn't naturally organised when I was younger, so I had to work hard to set up fool-proof systems that meant nothing falls through the cracks. You need to be sure that your diary is up-to-date with all the upcoming work days you have on, your messages and emails are replied to in a timely manner and your kit is organised and ready to go, sometimes at a moment's notice.

Imagine getting booked on a makeup job and putting it in your calendar on the wrong day, or with the wrong start time. It's extremely hard to replace a makeup artist at short notice so you could end up costing one of your clients or photographers hundreds or thousands of dollars from a simple error of inputting it in your calendar. These things matter!

Calendar

This goes without saying, but your calendar is hugely important for accurate info about upcoming work. Make sure you always carefully input confirmed shoot days or potential holds for workdays as soon as they come in so you don't forget. Schedules are forever shifting and changing so you need to update as new dates arrive or change.

Task Manager on your Phone

I know I mentioned how much I love lists, but keeping track of all the small details of answering messages and emails, what needs updating on your website, creating briefs and mood boards for upcoming jobs, as well as chasing PRs, receiving and properly storing hi-res images from photographers, staying connected with your network... the To Do list is never-ending so having a system to keep track of what you need to do each day is vital.

I don't know how people manage without using a task manager app, I think they're a godsend. It's best to have a task manager app on your phone so you can keep on top of your tasks even on a shoot day. Well known task manager apps include Todoist and OmniFocus. Most have a free version so you can see if you like it and then a monthly fee of around $4 or $5 USD a month. They are worth their weight in gold.

MANAGING YOUR KIT

Whilst buying makeup to replace things in your kit might sound like pure fun, it's actually quite a lot of work once you start shooting regularly. It's vital that you create not only a good, usable system to organise your makeup kit but also a system for replacing things when you run low on a job. The reason makeup artists carry so much makeup to any given job is you need to be prepared and organised for any eventuality. And that means thinking about and organising what you will need on that day, ahead of time.

As you go you will figure out what you need in your kit, but you can't afford to forget that you need to buy new loose powder, or nail polish remover, or that your body makeup has run out when you're on-set. Thus you need to keep track of what's in your kit and what you either might have taken out or has been used up. Every makeup artist has a different system for how they like their kit to be organised but it's something to be aware of, and to start thinking about at the beginning of your career.

PREPARATION FOR WORK

Due to the fact that almost every job is different, with different talent, a different crew, and in a new location, having the time to prepare for work and the systems in place to do it quickly and efficiently is key.

Before each job you need:

- To make sure your brushes are washed and dry.
- Your kit is cleaned and sanitised and ready for the requirements of that job (depending on the talent, the number of people you will be making up, the type of makeup you will be doing and so on).
- You might need to do some research into the team you are shooting with or the talent if you haven't worked with them before.
- You have confirmed you have received your call sheet for the next day. This usually arrives the day before the job, sometimes on the evening before the job.

- You need to know how you will get to the job, in good time to start setting up prior to your start time (also called your 'Call Time'.)
- It's always a good idea to double-check the location details on the call sheet, not just to figure out where you'll be going but to confirm that you have the correct address – for instance, that the postcode on the call sheet matches what is on the map location. On rare occasions there might be a mistake with this on the call sheet and it makes for a very stressful morning if you haven't checked beforehand!

Transport Apps

Citymapper is a transport app available in many capital cities and is a fantastic tool to show you all the options of getting somewhere, including how long it will take to get there. It has live updates so it can also tell you if there are unexpected problems with your intended mode of transport, such as train delays or road closures.

FITTING IT ALL IN

This is also something worth thinking about ahead of time, as being a makeup artist means you have a lot less control of your schedule than someone in a 9-5 office job. Shoots can come in at the last minute (sometimes the day before, although this is fairly rare), so the more organised and ready to go you are, the better able you are to utilise the time you have available in any week. It's also less stressful and you can figure out how you will fit in all the things that you want to get done around your shooting schedule.

Regular Check-ins

I think a Monthly and Weekly check-in of what you have to do is quite important, as it allows you to plan ahead for your all-important portfolio building work, as well as networking and client meetings, plus general life stuff such as exercise, doctor visits, family events and other things that need to be managed. Everyone reading this has different circumstances and thus different amounts of time available to build their career, but the most important thing is to keep your eye on the long-term horizon of where you want your career to go, and yet also focus on the next tasks you need to do to get you there.

CHAPTER 13

Managing your Health

Makeup is a very physical job. One makeup artist I assisted commented that you have to start thinking of your body like an athlete's, because if your body isn't working right, it's simple - you won't be able to work. Then you'll be unwell and also have no money coming in. An ounce of prevention is worth a pound of cure so getting into good habits will benefit you enormously over the course of your career.

So, I consider the very basics of good health to be:

- Eating well
- Exercising on your days off, preferably a form of exercise that strengthens the muscles and the core like Pilates or yoga
- Mindfulness practices like meditation to quieten the mind
- Getting sufficient sleep, rest and relaxation
- Getting regular holidays (this can be surprisingly hard to do as there will always be more great jobs coming in that you don't want to miss out on.)
- Drinking plenty of water each day (2-3 litres a day is ideal.)

All of these good practices will go a long way to keeping you fit and healthy and ready to work. Remember it's a physical job so you need to be in peak shape to keep up with the demands of your ever-evolving makeup career.

When I was younger and assisting, I lived literally the opposite of this advice. It was like I'd taken this guide and then set fire to it - eating badly, working super long hours, not exercising consistently and year after year working and juggling childcare and portfolio shoots along with my assisting commitments. So please forgive me if you feel like I'm stating the obvious to you, as this wasn't at all obvious to me at the beginning of my makeup career - which is why I feel like it's worth saying to you now. Also, the younger you are the more physical punishment your body can withstand, but if you want to have a long career in makeup and be healthy as well, it's best to set things up correctly at the beginning.

For years when I was assisting, I was lugging literally hundreds of kilos of makeup (sometimes two giant suitcases on the Eurostar to Paris), drinking all the tea and coffee all day long (for energy, since I hardly had any) with sugar and milk, wine on my days off, eating gluten and dairy (both of which it turns out I'm allergic to) and pastries and Coca-Cola and generally treating my body like a small but mostly uncomplaining wastebin. I did have terrible insomnia and then my health fell apart eventually, leading to auto-immune problems, operations and an enforced break from makeup whilst I healed.

I'm also always speaking to older creatives with at least a couple of decades of experience who have back or hip or knee problems, and given that our job involves standing all day, bending into awkward positions to apply makeup in random studio chairs and dragging suitcases of makeup all over town, I know why. The longer you do makeup for, the more important it is to have good health habits, both physically and mentally.

LOOKING AFTER YOUR HEALTH AT WORK

- Sit down where possible. Not to the point that you're sprawled all over the furniture but let yourself rest when you can. When you're assisting it's difficult as it's not a great look for an assistant to be sitting when the artist

you're assisting is standing, but certainly on your own jobs, perch where possible.
- Have good shoes that allow you to stand and walk, and run, when necessary. Bad quality shoes will bite you on the ass, as well as the instep, over the years.
- Be as comfortable as you can on location. If you're shooting outdoors and it's going to be cold and perhaps wet (hello shooting in England for most of the year), you need a good quality waterproof jacket, wellies, hats, nice warm gloves, umbrellas - all the gear to protect yourself when you're out because location can be much more physically demanding than shooting in the studio. For hot climates, sunglasses, sunhats and plenty of sunscreen will prevent you from getting sunstroke, which I have had after one of my first jobs on a yacht on Sydney Harbour and it was horrible, thank you very much.
- In terms of transporting your makeup, choose a great quality suitcase that has good wheels and rolls with ease (Burton Snowboard bags seem to the bag of choice in the industry at the moment as they have great wheels designed to handle most terrains.) I have bags in different sizes so I can scale my kit up or down depending on the job. Male grooming is going to require a lot less product than a beauty shoot with lots of looks and three models.
- I know everyone waffles on about how amazing yoga is, but it is. Seriously. If you can't find the time or money to go to a yoga class, Yoga with Adriene on YouTube has literally hundreds of videos that you can do for free at home. Yoga will help strengthen your body for your makeup work and calm your mind and just generally make you feel awesome.
- Try to live as near to where most of your work is if you can, or somewhere with decent transport links. Makeup is not a job where it's easy to call in sick, or tell the team that you can't make your job that day because your train has been delayed or cancelled or you got snowed in. Have back-up

transport plans in mind for when things do sometimes go wrong.
- Manage what you say yes to if you find you are getting exhausted. For me that means cutting right down on editorial if I'm feeling burnt out. I focus on paid jobs only in those times, so I can get my energy back up again. That's the beauty of being a freelance makeup artist, you can choose when, where and with whom you work. (Mostly.)
- Take rest days and prioritise looking after yourself. I'm not great at this, but I am getting a lot better. I have been learning that if I make sure that the basics of fresh air, good food, adequate sleep and regular time to laugh and see friends and family are covered, I am not only much happier, but my work gets better.
- Meditation is another great self-care practice that people talk about, with good reason. All sorts of research are being done at present into meditation and its benefits, but it calms the mind, reduces stress and anxiety and apparently increases your working spatial memory by 30% (who knew?) There is a wonderful meditation expert called Tara Brach (she can be found online at Tarabrach.com) that I point people to that has hundreds of free guided meditations if you want to get started on it.

DECANT YOUR KIT

Last but by no means least, decant your kit as much as you humanly can without impacting the performance of the product. Keep your kit as small and compact as possible.

Lipsticks, cream blushes and eyeshadows can all go in palettes. There are a million depotting and decanting videos on YouTube and as your kit grows, work on reducing the weight of your overall makeup as you build your kit. Don't wait until you have a back injury to start decanting.

If you really want to nerd out on decanting, check out @theartistarsenal on Instagram for inspiration. Muji is a great shop for palettes and little jars and bottles to decant into, as are specialist theatrical and film makeup shops which can be found in most cities around the world. Amazon and eBay are also good places to look for mini jars and containers.

Whilst there is almost nothing quite as painful in life as cutting up a Pat McGrath or Tom Ford lipstick, believe me when I say the incremental improvements in how much weight you carry every day to work outweigh that pain.

MANAGING BURNOUT

You will come to inflection points in your career when you just feel exhausted. Tired from lugging your kit, from doing jobs you have outgrown, from back to back pre-dawn starting times and physically drained from the hours of standing.

This unfortunately is part and parcel of the job. If there is a Makeup Artist Land filled with unicorns and rainbows where every job pays what you would like, isn't miles away from your home and gives you great new images for your portfolio and Instagram every time you shoot, please send me an email because I'd love to hear about it.

This book is NOT designed to lull you into a sense of false security that pursuing your dreams will mean you are always fulfilled. Every job has its tough points, and tough times, and knowing that those times happen to everyone periodically, and you aren't a weirdo for feeling that way is one of the most important things.

Especially if becoming a makeup artist has been a long-held dream for you, it can feel a bit confronting when you get to one of these sticky places I'm talking about and you realise you're feeling a little bit down about your career choice. In almost every case, it will pass. It might take some time (a few weeks, a couple of months perhaps) where you feel rather dejected about how things are going, but you will almost always get your mojo back.

I know from assisting so many different, amazing makeup artists over the years that this is just one of the inevitable ebbs and flows that goes with the territory.

My advice on this topic is the same as it would be to any other burnt-out person, focus on looking after yourself. Perhaps scale back your work commitments for a bit if you can – luckily as creatives it's easier to say no to work than if you're in an office full-time. Review your budget and spend less so you can earn less for a while if need be, and make sure your physical health is good by eating right, exercising and getting sufficient sleep. You know the drill. See some friends, do your laundry, and just try and step away from the makeup and Instagram as long as you can to get your chutzpah back. It will come back! And if it doesn't, that's a bigger conversation that you need to have with yourself which you can't have when you're standing for hours on set, and mentally feeling worn out.

If the unhappy feelings around work aren't resolving in a few weeks, take a holiday or a mini break if possible, to give you some space and thinking time. If that's just not on the cards, at least go and enjoy some green space like a park in your city for as long as you can. Journaling, hot baths, dog walks and time with friends and family are all key to self-nurture and also self-discovery. It's hard to feel good about anything if you are physically and mentally exhausted.

It's really just about recognising that these times do come along in every makeup artist's career, even the most successful. They do resolve in most cases. Don't forget that as a makeup artist and working for yourself, it can sometimes be lonely, and you don't have co-workers to discuss these times. If you're lucky you might have some makeup artist friends you can talk to, but sometimes the road can be hard. Your family may not always understand your choices and really 'get' the sometimes difficult reality of being a makeup artist. That's OK, but it does mean you have to support yourself physically, mentally and emotionally when times feel challenging. Always remember, this is a marathon, not a sprint.

CHAPTER 14

Getting an Agent

Creative management agencies are agencies that represent artists in the beauty and fashion industries – such as makeup artists, hair stylists, manicurists, photographers, stylists and prop stylists, and help look after their careers.

A good agent is worth their weight in gold, providing invaluable career advice, introductions to clients, putting you forward for upcoming jobs (both advertising and editorial), and handling the day to day administration, leaving you to be able to focus on your makeup. They get bookings for the creatives they represent, do invoicing, chase late payments, arrange taxis and travel and make sure all the details of every job they are working on is organised.

But most vitally of all, they can help steer your career and take it to the next level. They will introduce you to bigger clients and give indispensable advice on your portfolio and social media marketing and also provide access to their industry contacts, both locally and often internationally. In exchange they are paid a commission both from the clients booking the talent, and from the creatives they represent. This fee structure varies from country to country but usually ranges from between 20-40%.

BENEFITS OF HAVING AN AGENT

I get asked 'How do I get an agent' aaaallll the time, and many creatives, not just makeup artists, treat this like the Holy Grail of their professional life. It is an amazing feeling getting an agent (I'm not going to lie) and it's also an inflection point in your career – from that point on you will be considered for jobs that you might not have been prior to getting an agent, you command more money, and you have an ally to support you in the sometimes lonely world of being a freelancer. In addition, having an agent is an endorsement of your work. Because someone in the business has chosen to endorse you, a client might be more likely to for significant jobs.

Most powerfully of all, they negotiate fees on your behalf which few people like to do for themselves. They will also have a lot more experience at this. So not only are you being put forward for bigger jobs as the result of having an agent, but you can also (in theory) earn more money on all your jobs, although this is something you will need to work out with your agent regarding how your existing clients will be managed.

NEGATIVES OF HAVING AN AGENT

It can be cheaper for your clients if you don't have an agent, and a client may be 'scared' of agency fees. However, a good agent will usually negotiate the agency fee together with your payment, so it's done in a way that doesn't feel separate. Or it can be worked out so that your agent takes the commission out of your usual rate, meaning an existing client doesn't end up paying a higher fee. Thus, it may not end up costing your current clients more if you become represented by an agent.

Without an agent, you also keep all of the money that you receive for jobs, and don't have to pay a commission to anyone else. But you have to weigh up the time and energy you then spend doing all of the things that they would be able to help you with, so that is something else to consider.

Finally, there is the risk that an agency can go bust unexpectedly taking a lot of your hard earned money with it - which has happened with a few of the bigger global agencies in recent years.

However, at some point in your career progression I think you have to decide about your long-term strategy and what you need to get to the next stage as a makeup artist. If you want to access higher levels of the industry, you will need help and guidance to get you there.

Once I got my agent in London, she went through my book with a ruthless eye (much better than mine!) and we re-organised my portfolio and website. Then she was booking me appointments to meet with new clients and photographers and magazine editors. Soon I was being considered for editorial in much higher level magazines than I had been able to access previously, such as Harper's Bazaar and Vogue editorials, as well as red carpet makeup for the BAFTAS. Suddenly the pool of work I was now able to attain with an agent was much bigger than the level I had been able to reach on my own.

TIPS FOR GETTING AN AGENT

Firstly, don't rush it! It's a big and important decision so you want to spend some time doing the necessary fact-finding beforehand. Think hard and do a lot of research before taking on an agent, as the agent you choose will significantly impact the course of your career. You want an agent who you feel has your best interests at heart, so you need to meet with quite a few to find out who you like.

Have a good think about what you want your agent to do for you. Some agencies focus mainly on handling the administration side of things, and others will give you advice on what you should be focusing on next for the development of your career. How involved do you want them to be in decisions about the jobs that you do, or regarding fees, or your portfolio? So it's about finding what you require and what a prospective agent can offer you to find the right agent to work with. Some agencies are one size fits all but a good one will offer different services to different artists depending on what they need.

Reflect on what type of work you do, and what type of work you'd like to do. Are you keen to mainly do commercial/advertising work? Then choose an agent that does mainly commercial work. If you want to focus on very high fashion, there are only a handful of agencies in the world that do this sort of work, and it could take you years to join them, but it's worth holding out and waiting to join the agencies that will help you to access that part of the industry, if that's what you want.

Different agencies have different strengths and styles and may not look like they represent who/what you want to be, but they might be open to it when you talk to them. This applies in all cities with creative agencies – each agency will tend to have a particular aesthetic or type of creative that they represent. Some are more lifestyle based or have a focus on interiors or food styling or beauty clients. Some have a kids' brand focus or might have an edge with celebrities or music personalities. It's up to you to thoroughly research each agency and work out what direction is best suited to you and your work.

Once you have decided what you need in an agent, and researched the agencies in your local city, then speak to as many agencies as possible. A lot of it will develop as you have these initial meetings as it's also about the personality fit with you and your potential agency. Your agent will be someone you speak to almost every day, usually multiple times a day, so I think it's super important to make it someone that you're happy to do that with.

In the agency meetings, ask how they like to do things and whether they can accommodate how you would like to do things. Think about what you don't want as well as what you do want in an agent. Also, worth noting is that some agencies will expect you to do both hair and makeup, and some are happy for you to do makeup only, but definitely check that out first in your initial conversations with them.

HOW DO I KNOW I'M READY FOR AN AGENT?

This is quite a difficult one to answer, but you will start to get a feel for when you think you might be ready to approach agencies. To help you make the decision, spend some time really comparing the level and quality of your work with the people that they represent. Do you have clients of a similar level to the artists that they already represent? Are you doing editorial in the same level of magazines? Are there other artists in the industry that you consider either peers or are more junior than you who are getting taken on by agencies? Do you have an aesthetic that will fit well with the agency you're considering? You need to keep working on your portfolio until it's at a similar level, and your makeup is of a standard that you feel you could confidently work at the level of the clients that they look after.

The other thing to note about getting an agent is that a lot of agents won't be interested in you joining the agency if you don't have a client list to bring to them already, so you need to build your client list and your portfolio on your own before you approach them. However, some agents really enjoy building and nurturing someone's career from the beginning. Either way it's important to build your own network and work together as a team.

It is possible to get an agent without having a great deal of work or experience; but this is the exception rather than the rule. Sometimes an agent might just see something in you that they really like and be happy to take you on without you having a huge client list already. It's not just the makeup work, it's also about how your personality fits with both the booker and the agency.

Agent Emma Davies had this to say on how she chooses to take on a new artist: "When I look at taking on a new artist, apart from being good at what they do, (even if they don't have that much work to show), I ask the people I know who have worked with that artist to get honest feedback. I want to know if they're honest, diligent, hardworking, trustworthy, great at their job and nice to be around."

Whilst it's a good idea to have an agency you would like to join in future in mind, the best thing to do is to just get your head down and focus on producing the best work that you can. Thus, when you do get that meeting in with them to speak to them about joining their roster of artists, it will be a no-brainer for them to say yes as they can see that you have clients and that you're already working well. You need to bring work to your agency as well as them bringing your work to you – it should be a win/win relationship. The ideal is of course a 50/50 split but it depends on where you're at, naturally.

Before the Agency Meeting

I don't need to tell you this, but before your initial contact with them, make sure all your marketing is up to date – your website, Instagram, LinkedIn and things like email footers should all be current and as professional as possible.

Also make sure you have been following the agency for at least a couple of months on Instagram – it's hard to argue convincingly you want to join a particular agency if they check your Instagram (which they will) and you're not even following them. Being regularly present on their Instagram feeds also would be useful, so that when the time comes to initially contact them, your name might hopefully ring a bell with the person opening your email.

Spend some time crafting a good message and of course within the body of the email, include good (working!) links to your website and Instagram. A PDF of your latest work as well as a short, concise list of your current clients and editorial would be good as well so the person opening the email (who don't forget probably gets many of these emails a day) can see immediately why you would be an asset for their agency. Keep it simple - you don't want to send too many PDFs or attachments as you can always send them extra information, such as a full client list, if there's any interest from your initial email. Be polite, friendly and having knowledge of who they represent is always helpful.

Timing

Timing is very important. If you have an amazing new advertising campaign coming out, or a beautiful editorial in a great magazine about to land, wait until it's out before you go in to see them.

Certain times of the year are better to approach an agency as well. The times to AVOID are:

- December as it's coming up on Christmas and people are winding up the year and can be distracted with Christmas parties and festivities.
- January, as so many other people do it at that time as they are thinking of fresh starts for the new year.
- Summertime as your email might get missed as staff at the agency take their summer holidays.

But if you have been recommended by someone else at the agency or a mutual contact at any time of the year, then you should obviously follow up immediately.

This goes without saying, but it's best not to send representation request emails over a weekend or late on a Friday night - as Emma Davies says, "a good agent is never 'off' but it does look like you might not respect their space so doesn't give a good starting impression." Also, a message sent over the weekend/evening might be seen and then forgotten about. If you do have to email over the weekend, acknowledge it, apologise and follow up nicely.

It's a plus to have worked with some of the people at that agency if possible as well – it shows you're already in the sphere of the agency's business so easier for them to imagine you working with their clients.

IS IT POSSIBLE TO BE SUCCESSFUL WITHOUT AN AGENT?

Yes, I do think you can have some level of success without an agent. Especially now with social media, the ball is in your court more than ever in how you promote yourself. So don't let NOT having an agent stop you from hustling as hard as you can to get yourself working.

It has never been easier to market yourself online, and I know many makeup artists who are very happy without an agent. There are some people who have never had an agent and they've had long and successful careers.

The mechanics of managing yourself are actually fairly easy, at least if you currently aren't shooting every day. It's more the volume of work involved in managing yourself as you get busier and busier which can become difficult. The more work you get, and the more successful you become, the harder it is to keep on top of the daily logistics of shooting every day, and that way, my friends, leads to burnout. It's also about getting to that next level of your career which makes having an agent a game changer.

SECTION FIVE

Dealing with different life circumstances

I ALREADY HAVE A FULL-TIME JOB – CAN I TRANSITION TO BECOMING A MAKEUP ARTIST?

I speak to many, many would-be makeup artists who are currently in a full-time job and are dreaming of quitting the corporate 9-5 life for a career in makeup. If this is you, you're in a great position, because you already have a job that pays you regular income. This can then be used to help you fund your makeup dream, but you will need to be both patient and organised. Lots of people in the fashion industry also have other weekday jobs nowadays as the market for creatives is quite saturated, so it's actually a good time to make a transition as more shoots happen at the weekends. In the past it was harder to juggle a full-time job and makeup as fewer shoots would happen at the weekend.

Don't forget this is the long game you are playing – think of the tortoise, not the hare. My best advice would be to keep your current job whilst you build up your makeup work at weekends, or when you have free time available. Especially in the current uncertain climate, I would be very remiss to tell you to quit your job and launch yourself into the unknown.

I can't stress enough how important it is to be able to support yourself whilst you build your makeup career, and the beauty of already having a full-time job is that you already have a good income coming in. The trick is how you will leverage your spare time (which you probably don't have much of, if you're in full-time employment) and get your makeup career rolling. It's not easy, but it is possible.

If you are really serious about transitioning to becoming a makeup artist, you need to:

- Get clear about your expenses and if you can reduce them down, work on that. It will help immeasurably.
- Build your makeup kit over time, so make sure you have a monthly Makeup Budget allowing you to work on this whilst you still have a regular paycheck coming in.

- You also need to save a good stash of money so you have savings for when you go full-time into makeup, and for when times are lean in future. This happens periodically in every freelancer's life, no matter how talented you are. The economy goes up and down, clients come and go, the type of work you do can go in and out of fashion, pandemics unfortunately do happen. That's why you always have a good Emergency Fund to keep you going through the inevitable financial winter that will arrive one day.
- Practice in your spare time. On your friends, family, your partner, anyone you can get in your chair is great. Every age, every ethnicity, every gender, with all different skins and skin conditions. People with allergies and vitiligo and wrinkles and acne, you want them all so you can practice working on every type of skin and test out your skincare and foundations to ensure you're completely confident about how they perform. And if you are struggling to get people to practice on, which I found was an issue for me when my friends started having babies and I had a baby myself, practice on yourself.
- Your new weekend side hustle could be a makeup business that you can manage outside of your corporate job. Build up a wedding business or do makeup counter work at weekends or in the Christmas period when they need extra staff. Private clients who need makeup at weekends for events would also work. Whilst you are doing this, you are getting to grips with your expenses, getting practice, building your kit, creating your portfolio and stashing cash, as well as giving you time by taking baby steps into your new career to deciding whether being a full-time makeup artist is really what you want.
- You could also look at focusing on building your portfolio at the weekends, by contacting photographers and other creatives. Unfortunately, these shoots won't pay you money, but having a good portfolio is a necessity to bring in more work. At some point, it will be time to think about

making the leap into full-time makeup. You will feel like you are ready to try being a makeup artist on your own once your expenses and the money you have coming in from makeup are in alignment.

It won't be easy, but big things in life never are. And you have the peace of mind that a steady paycheck coming in brings, and you are making the transition in a responsible and sensible way. Once you know you could live on what your makeup business provides, then you are probably ready to make the jump into fully freelance life.

Also think about whether you're prepared to put in the kind of time it may take, and the sacrifice of your weekends and evenings – deep down you may think that sounds like it could take too long, or be too much work, and that's totally fine! Better to know that now than four years in.

One of my main motivations for writing this book was because I had to learn all these things by trial and error, and if I'd known what the options were in greater detail ahead of time, I know I would have done things differently. So at least with this book you have the information up front rather than years and thousands of dollars spent on makeup down the road.

WHAT IF I HAVE ALREADY LEFT MY JOB TO BECOME A MAKEUP ARTIST?

If you have already thrown caution to the wind and have left your full-time job to do makeup, there's a path forward for you too. Or perhaps you have lost your job and decided now is the time to really test out your dream of being a makeup artist.

The information in the section above applies to you too, regardless of whether you can currently focus on makeup 100% or have another part-time job you are doing in the meanwhile to support yourself. Your focus should be on having as much time as possible to devote to your makeup, keeping your expenses low and shooting to get your portfolio/clients together.

Just work as quickly and efficiently as you can to build your portfolio, especially if you have some free time at your disposal before you need to start earning money again. Structure your days to get the most benefit out of them possible. Even if you are only available one or two days a week for makeup, you can still make plenty of progress over the timeframe of a year.

HOW DO I BRING IN WORK WHEN THE INDUSTRY IS QUIET?

Sometimes there just isn't much work around, or if there is, you don't know about it and you aren't getting it. This is just part of the gig of being a makeup artist, and if you can't stop yourself having a nervous breakdown whenever the industry slows down, this job is probably not for you.

What has helped me immeasurably with this is from thinking of everyone that I've assisted over the years, and yes, even they also have quiet periods. Thus if someone who I think is one of the best in the world has times when they aren't that busy, then you can expect periods when your work offers are not that plentiful too.

The trick is to know that those times come, they always get better and you will always slightly freak out when you aren't getting booked for a few days. Know that everyone in the industry thinks occasionally that they will never work again when it's been quiet for a period of time.

Analyse What's Working – and What Isn't

The first thing to do is analyse what's going on. Look at your marketing efforts. Look at all your paid jobs – where did they come from? Can you get more of those? Can you find more of the types of people who referred you for previous jobs?

I can't begin to tell you what an eye opener this is. Look at the last few months of work you've done as quite often you might find you're getting work from unexpected people or places. Then do more of whatever is working for you, and less of what isn't. This analysis can take a few hours but is well worthwhile doing on a periodic basis.

Analyse Your Portfolio

Look at your portfolio and all your marketing. Are there any gaps in your portfolio? Have you got new editorial shoots out or about to come out that could shift things for you? Do you need more beauty editorial in your book? More kids? Celebrities? Male grooming? Does your website need an update?

Analyse Your Time

Also analyse how you are spending your time. How many appointments are you getting? How many of these are useful? How many responses are you getting to your emails – are you aiming too high with the people you are contacting? Are you aiming too low? Are there shoots that you are doing that aren't providing enough value for the hours you put into them?

Quiet periods are a great time to step back and look at whether you're happy about what you're doing, the direction your career is headed in and what type of work you'd like to have more of in future.

Reach Out to Your Network

Touch base with your network to see what the other creatives you know are up to, and it's the perfect time to reach out to some new photographers and stylists and make new connections. If you put some effort into understanding why your work has slowed down and use these periods to meet a fresh batch of creatives, I guarantee it won't be long before you're so busy working that you'll be dreaming of having time to do your laundry and get a haircut. And sometimes of course it's a quiet time for the industry in your city as a whole, but you will get a feel for this by reaching out to your network and finding out (discreetly) if the other creatives you know are equally quiet.

Emergency Fund

This is also when your Emergency Fund comes in totally handy to tide you over, and your recent calculations about how much you need to live on when you did your budgeting allows you to see how long you can get by if the lean weeks continue. If they go on too long, you'll need to start that part-time job search, but at least having thought about it in advance you don't have to panic with the uncertainty of not knowing if/when that may be on the cards.

The quiet period will move into the rear-view mirror of your life as it always does, and you'll be back to your usual busy self eventually. And when you do, you'll have a pristine underwear drawer and a perfectly organised kit to enjoy and feel smug that you used your downtime wisely.

I CAN'T PAY MY BILLS THIS MONTH, WHAT SHOULD I DO?

This won't ever be a problem for you, will it, because you will have a fully stocked Emergency Fund! I'm going to be annoying and say it again - the better you get at money management, the easier you will find the whole process of becoming a makeup artist. But the longer you don't work for, means the bigger the Emergency Fund that you need. And even a really good Emergency Fund won't last forever.

The first thing you need to do is not freak out. Panicking is not helpful, and worst makes you feel desperate which without being all cosmic and LA on you really does seem to repel money and work opportunities.

The best state of mind is to feel mentally relaxed, or as much as you can be, and to think productively about solutions. Sometimes it can be a lean month, or it can be even longer, so it's a good idea to have a time limit in mind on how long you can wait before cracking on with getting some other type of paid work.

When I told you about keeping an eye on and understanding your expenses, this is why – if you look at the data you can sometimes anticipate this slow period is coming, and if it is you may need to think about taking on a part-time job to keep you going and wait for the tide to turn on your makeup work. Obviously the earlier you can see this coming the better, rather than when you've just cleaned out your bank account buying new clothes. if you can see yourself starting to eat into your Emergency Fund that is a warning sign that you need to do something different to get some more commercial clients in.

Touch base with everyone you know, and try and do some new editorial shoots, to get fresh images for your portfolio and your Instagram. Seeking out details of companies that do lots of e-commerce shoots is ideal, and there may well be different people you haven't spoken to for a bit who may be able to help you get some paid work in.

Some people look at doing a bit of assisting as well as that can bring in some money, although as I mentioned before a lot of makeup assisting work is free so I wouldn't want this to be my only Plan B.

But let's just put you in the worst-case scenario for a moment – let's say work has been totally dead for three months, you're coming to the end of your emergency savings and the crickets are chirping in your bank account and there is still not much work around.

The ideal scenario is at least a month ago you would have anticipated this and started looking for something for yourself in terms of work, which could be literally anything that pays your bills. Working on a makeup counter, doing brides at the weekend, or makeup for private clients are all makeup related options I encourage you to look at as a fallback, well in advance of needing it. Working in a café, a shop, or selling things on eBay, waitressing or Deliveroo, working on reception, setting up an Etsy shop, or babysitting are all potential options. Basically whatever you can do that takes as little time as possible so you can still be available when your makeup work picks up again. Even taking a full-time job somewhere for a few months until you build up your financial stash again is an option.

Get shooting, get posting on your Instagram, reach out and make as many connections as you can, be good to yourself by exercising and eating right and just be patient as these times do pass.

How Long Should I Wait?

In a periodic downturn, everyone has a time limit on how long they are prepared to wait for work to pick up again, and it's good to have an idea of how long you can last with little paid work coming in. Just to let you know that generally it's only a few weeks or a couple of months that work sometimes gets really quiet, but the other consideration is mentally how long YOU are prepared to wait for things to improve. Three months? Six months? A year? Only you can know how long that is, but if you will be miserable with the financial and lifestyle changes that you have made by cutting expenses or changing your living arrangements, doing it for months and years on end isn't what I would recommend. If your dream to be a makeup artist is making you unhappy for long periods of time, it might be necessary to rethink the dream.

This is time to seriously assess how long you're going to put into becoming a makeup artist before it could be time to call it a day and look for full-time work again. I say this because there have been periods when I had to stop for a while (with my muscle injury) when I thought I would have to stop completely, and I found NOT thinking about it was actually more stressful than dealing with the issue and facing my fears straight on. As it turned out I was able to go back to work eventually after a break, but not knowing whether I could continue as a makeup artist was the most stressful thing for me.

I'VE HAD A CAREER SETBACK – WHAT DO I DO TO SNAP OUT OF IT?

Everyone has points in their career when they've taken a few knocks in a row. Maybe some editorials that you put a lot of work into didn't end up getting published for reasons that have nothing to do with your makeup, or a regular client has decided to start working with someone else. Or maybe you're frustrated that your makeup skills aren't at the level that you would like, for the jobs that you're wishing you could do. Maybe the rate you're being offered for a job is lower than it was, or some work you've done hasn't been as well received as you might have hoped.

All these things do happen, and the most important thing is to get back on your feet and not let them throw you off your stride for too long. It's fine to take a few days off to recover mentally and re-assess what's needed to get back on track, but don't spend too long dwelling on it. As long as you're still generally happy with your overall career choice of being a makeup artist, then don't sweat a setback for too long.

The best way I've found to get through this period is to get back to work on building your portfolio with new shoots as quickly as possible. As ever, look at what the gaps might be in your portfolio, or where you think you would like to push your career to next and get on with planning shoots to make that happen. Getting straight back to doing the work will make you forget about what went wrong, and allow you to keep trying out things until they go right again. By giving yourself a new project to focus on it allows you to push through to the next phase of your career and get back on track.

HOW DO I COME BACK TO MAKEUP WORK AFTER A BREAK?

Maybe you've taken time out to have a baby, or maybe you've had a work injury, a family crisis or you've moved countries. Getting back to work under any of those circumstances is challenging. I know this very well having hopped back and forth between London and Sydney for over a decade, and it's particularly difficult when you are moving between two very different markets (in my case, Sydney is more commercial, and London is more fashion based, so the portfolio I needed for each place was almost completely different.)

Since every market is distinct and depending on how long you've been out of that particular market, or if it's a new city for you, you may need to pretty much re-shoot your portfolio.

This can feel overwhelming at first, but it's not impossible. Like anything, just start by going step by step. Firstly, you should start by getting in touch with your old network, all the people you used to work with in that city to touch base and let them know you're back in town and ready to shoot. But don't take it personally if they don't all jump up and down to give you work. People move on, they are busy and if your portfolio is out of date or not right for that market it makes it a hard sell to a client on behalf of the person recommending you, even if they do already know and like you and your work.

My advice is to start contacting people and shooting again within this market as quickly as you can to build a new network, as well as keeping in touch with your older contacts. It will also give you updated images for your Instagram and portfolio to show people you're back in the game and available to shoot. Luckily you already have a good CV of photographers and magazine titles for that particular city so it should be easier to get working with new people.

If it's a completely new place for you, just spend some time researching who is working in that market currently. Do your Instagram research, then start following and liking people's posts and then begin contacting them to shoot as soon as you can.

Again, it's not going to be a magic success overnight but slow, steady and consistent contact with people and reaching out on a regular basis will eventually get you working. But it's up to you to get the ball rolling.

HOW DO I MANAGE MAKEUP WORK IF I HAVE KIDS?

This is a great question and I get asked it all the time. As someone who has raised a child whilst working as a makeup artist, I know it's not easy but it's not out of the question either.

Working Whilst Pregnant

First off, everyone's situation is obviously different. Some people can work all through their pregnancies almost up to their due date and be fine, I was so nauseous that I couldn't work at all and I found out I was pregnant when I first started assisting — not ideal timing!

It really varies from person to person — depending on your physical strength, your health, the baby's health and obviously your childcare situation when the baby is born.

Please be sensible when working when you're pregnant. No heavy lifting of giant suitcases full of makeup - watch how much kit you're carrying, and just take it easy if you need to. Bring in assistants to help you whenever you can and perhaps focus on scaling back to just the most important or highest paying jobs. A happy, healthy mama and baby is the goal of any pregnancy, not an exhausted and run down one. Some people feel great for their whole pregnancy, in which case work away!

Again, the key to all of this is planning ahead, as much as you can. The most important thing if you want to keep working is quality childcare, so If you are thinking about having children, start looking into childcare places and options as soon as possible. I think before you get pregnant (if you're thinking of having kids soon, start looking in the next little while, in other words) is the best time for this, because sometimes you might want to move to help make childcare easier.

Family help is of course ideal for childcare, but many people don't have family nearby or able to assist. There is a wide range of childcare available in most countries ranging from the local council, to childminders to private day-care, or depending on the size of your house an au pair might be an option.

Nannies are great but obviously the most expensive alternative, however you could look at sharing a nanny with another family which brings the cost down considerably. All childcare can be expensive though, and depending on what your day rate is, you might find that what you are earning by working for a day is cancelled out by the cost of the childcare.

Due to this cost and the unpredictability of a makeup artist's schedule, some makeup artists decide to stay at home with their children when they're small, especially if they have more than one under school age child at home.

The fact that makeup artists only get booked usually a few days/weeks in advance, and that some jobs are very last minute, makes it very hard to know when you will need childcare. And most childcare or nurseries want you to book regular days ahead of time, which means you can often end up paying for childcare days that you aren't using to actually shoot. Thus, it can be a conundrum.

If you don't have daycare that is super flexible, you could also look at focusing on doing makeup at weekends such as weddings, and/or special occasion makeup, (so also mainly evenings and weekends), whilst your child/children are very young. Both weddings and private clients tend to pay well and means you can arrange for your partner or family to look after the child or get a babysitter as needed. Weddings in particular also tend to be booked reasonably far in advance which gives you plenty of time to find a babysitter for them.

It's so important to cherish that time with them as you only get it once and as the mother of a teenager, I can tell you the time goes fast. Take off as much time as you need and can afford because you don't get this time again. Work will always be there, but your baby won't always be a baby (even though they will of course, always be your baby.)

MAKEUP IS A SECOND CAREER FOR ME – AM I TOO OLD?

Personally, I'm not a believer in being "too old" or "too young" to do anything – if you're capable of doing the job, your age shouldn't matter. But if you do start makeup work as a more mature person, don't forget all the things that you bring to the job – so many transferable skills of punctuality, people skills, being sensible and able to master problems, which are all abilities you will have developed already in your years of working in other jobs.

All these things are great to have as a makeup artist and might well get you booked over a younger makeup artist with perhaps less life experience than you. Plus, if you don't do it, or at least give it a try, is it something you will always regret not doing? Just start in a sensible and considered way and see whether you like it. You should be able to answer your own question soon enough.

I DON'T LIVE IN A CAPITAL CITY – CAN I STILL BE A MAKEUP ARTIST?

Yes! As long as someone in the place that you live will pay to have makeup put on them, you can be a working makeup artist. In fact, being in a smaller city can be great as there tend to be less makeup artists already working to compete with - although the people who are already working in that industry might be hard to beat for jobs as they've often had a bit of a monopoly in that market for years.

The only time it would be difficult to do makeup is if you live in a very small town or in the countryside, but as long as you live within commuting distance of a reasonably sized town or city that has some scope for makeup work, you could do it.

Smaller Cities

If you are in a smaller city, pretty much all of them will have studios and photographers, private clients and brides, digital and branding agencies, small clothing brands, local magazines and influencers, corporate headshot work, department stores and clothing stores that do trunk shows (which is a sales event where a boutique or department store show their new merchandise to prospective buyers) and bridal boutiques and hairdressers you could partner with. Tons of opportunity to get started. Just think outside the square a bit and start connecting with people using Instagram in your local area in the realm of makeup that you want to work in.

In a smaller market I do have to say that doing both hair and makeup to a good standard is pretty much mandatory, so practicing your hair skills as well as your makeup skills is really important. In my hometown of Sydney, most of the jobs are still hair and makeup.

Capital Cities

However, if you do want to do very high fashion there are a few cities in the world where you need to be based. These cities are still New York, Paris and London. If you want to focus on celebrity, LA is the best place to be.

Being in the environment and around the people doing the type of work you aspire to is infinitely helpful, giving you opportunities to work on those jobs eventually. If you want to assist big makeup artists in fashion and you don't live where they work, you won't be able to.

That's why I moved away from Sydney, because even though it's a lovely city, I didn't feel I could do the type of makeup that I wanted to do and work with the publications and photographers that was my ultimate goal whilst I was living there. But you can always get your training done in a smaller city and then look at transitioning to somewhere else later on.

If you are thinking of moving, do your research into the prospective market, and try and spend as much time there as you can if possible before making the leap. There is an amazing website called Numbeo.com which allows you to see the cost of general living in all the world's cities relative to where you already live and is a total eye opener. Great for planning and budgeting your potential cost of living in a new city. It's much easier to transition and make the move if you have good data.

SECTION SIX
The road ahead

KEEPING UP YOUR CONFIDENCE – THE MENTAL GAME

I'm a huge believer in positive thinking, because without believing you can be successful at something, you won't be able to push through the difficulties that arise on your journey to your goal. But I also believe in being very realistic in life and having backup arrangements for when things don't go according to the original plan, as they inevitably do.

When we first dream of doing makeup the future is a perpetually rosy place where unicorns braid each other's manes and apply blush with little golden brushes, where Beyonce's agent is asking whether you're OK to do her makeup on the private jet whilst you fly overnight to her next event - only to find out that the future sometimes involves eating cereal for dinner and being unable to repair your car because you're waiting so long for a client to pay an invoice.

Sometimes being a makeup artist can be tough, very tough. But it shouldn't be tough forever either. Sometimes the makeup unicorns SHOULD be blessing you with their stardust magic, otherwise what's the point of the whole thing? Only you know how long you want to wait through the difficult periods, and letting you know you definitely aren't alone when those times strike.

We all have challenges in our lives and it's about being kind to yourself and understanding if you need to adjust course. Perhaps you will need to spend longer assisting than you initially anticipated. Perhaps you will need to take a part-time job to cover your expenses at some point. Perhaps you might need to focus on commercial work and no editorial for a period of time. Unavoidably as the path of your career unfolds it will require periods of personal change and growth that can be challenging to navigate.

The most important advice I can offer you is to understand that it's a long, slow process, and the journey is the destination. Always, always follow your passion – the FEELING you get when you do makeup. I know that sense of excitement so well and I know you do too, or you wouldn't still be reading. That amazing sense of elation when you're doing somebody's makeup and time has disappeared and it's just you and someone's face, creating something that wasn't there before – whether it's the lightest of natural makeups or a full transformation. It doesn't matter what type of makeup that you do, I know that you know that feeling.

If that emotion is still there, then you need to let the ebbs and flows, ups and downs of your makeup career just pass by. Focus on the next thing you need to do, understand what the next stage of your career might look like, keep where you want to be firmly in your mind and always be practicing your craft to get better. Put the hours in to improve, study the great fashion creatives who have gone before you and always have a mentality of pushing yourself to the next level.

The most important characteristic of a successful makeup artist is perseverance. It's about keeping on going when all the other ones stopped because it became too hard, or they lost the passion for it, or their personal circumstances changed, and they had to do something else. Always just keep going! Believe that it's possible as long as you still have that feeling and you still love it. Of course not every makeup artist will get the chance to do Vogue magazine, but that's fine. You can still have a wonderful, satisfying and enjoyable career, regardless of what type of makeup that you do, or where in the world that you live.

One of my favourite makeup artist stories is from Pat McGrath. In an April 2019 interview with British Vogue when speaking about the beginning of her career, she says: "I can very clearly remember coming home one day and crying in my living room after a really disappointing day of test shoots. I just felt so defeated and I thought to myself that I would just have to give up. And suddenly, the phone rang - it was a client I'd done a shoot for some two years ago, who'd remembered me and wanted to ask me to come to Japan for my first-ever tour."

"You really have to love beauty and fashion, because there's nothing easy about it. It can be the most wonderful job, to be able to work and play in cosmetics, but it will not be easy. Persevere! Don't stop. You really have to keep that joy because that's what keeps you going. Just go forth and continue. Make something new and really hone your craft. Find out who you are."

This is such brilliant advice. This is arguably the world's greatest makeup artist, and she came home and cried after a day of crappy test shoots when she first started out. Imagine if she'd given up that day! Thousands of great fashion images and iconic shoots wouldn't have happened if she had quit. If Pat McGrath says sometimes it's hard and you want to give up, then I think every makeup artist in the world can expect to feel like that at some point.

This is what this whole book is about, is to hopefully give you enough of the right information so that you can keep going, through the good times and the bad. To look at the process of becoming a makeup artist, which is not always easy and looks very daunting at the beginning, and decide whether to continue. To set yourself up for success rather than failing due to not having enough of the right knowledge, time, resources or money. And to demystify HOW to become a fashion makeup artist as no-one wants to tell you that very vital process of how you build a career.

You need to have confidence that you can get there, and you need to have ways to GET that confidence, even if you don't always feel it. No one feels confident all the time. Everyone looks at what their peers and competitors are doing, at jobs they lost and wished they had and feels low occasionally. But if you have a plan that you can follow, a virtuous spiral of work and how to get new work that builds on itself like a staircase, you know you have a roadmap to see you through.

The way to increase your confidence, to get your mojo back, is to do the work. To focus on that sensation you get when you do makeup, and to give yourself the next opportunity to experience it again. By methodically coming back to doing the work, your confidence will naturally build and it will get you back on track when you need it.

By doing this, every shoot and job you work on builds your experience and your practical skills as a makeup artist, as well as finding out more about yourself, how you like to work and the work you love to do. Needless to say you will need to work, hard, and it can take many years (even decades) to build a career that you are really happy with, but if it's what you think you want, the only way to know for sure is to begin.

YOU'RE ON YOUR WAY

If you've made it to the end of the book and knowing everything that is involved you're still excited about the journey to becoming a makeup artist, then you're ready to get started.

I have to say I literally cannot imagine doing anything else now – I just find it such a rewarding and fulfilling career that is full of challenges and extraordinary unique experiences that would be impossible to find doing anything else.

Putting makeup on people is addictive. Making them look and feel their best and giving them the confidence to face what might be their next challenge (a film premiere, a portrait shoot, or getting married) is such a privilege. Being creative and the fact that no two days are ever the same makes it endlessly exciting and challenging. The places you will see, the people you will meet and the growth that you will need to make in yourself to become the artist that you desire to be are never-ending.

If you are prepared to take the next steps on this makeup artist journey, I congratulate you, as the decision to take the leap is one of the hardest bits of the journey. If you could take anything away from this book though, it's that it's best that you make the leap in small, sensible increments, always keeping an eye on the business elements that will make it a financially viable career option. As the German poet Goethe famously said, "Whatever you can do or dream you can, begin it. Boldness has genius, power and magic in it."

Now you know the road to take, and whether it's for you, I wish you all the best as you journey down the exciting path to becoming a makeup artist.

Acknowledgements

With thanks to my agent, Emma Davies, who provided invaluable advice and whose vigorous editorial eye works as well on words as it does on pictures. Thanks to Kay Montano who is the greatest mentor and friend I could ask for – thank you for all the opportunities you have given me and not least for your friendship all these years. To Jude, who is the best parent I could ask for. And finally thank you to Boris and Finn who are my everything.

Printed in Great Britain
by Amazon